GCSE Edexcel
Core Science
Higher Workbook

This book is for anyone doing **GCSE Edexcel Core Science** at higher level.
It covers everything you'll need for your year 10 exams.

It's full of **tricky questions**... each one designed to make you **sweat**
— because that's the only way you'll get any **better**.

There are questions to see **what facts** you know. There are questions
to see how well you can **apply those facts**. And there are questions
to see what you know about **how science works**.

It's also got some daft bits in to try and make the whole
experience at least vaguely entertaining for you.

What CGP is all about

Our sole aim here at CGP is to produce the highest
quality books — carefully written, immaculately presented
and dangerously close to being funny.

Then we work our socks off to get them
out to you — at the cheapest possible prices.

Contents

B1 Topic 1 — Variation

Classification 1
More on Classification 2
Variation 3
Continuous and Discontinuous Variation 5
Extreme Environments 6
Natural Selection and Evidence for Evolution ... 8
Speciation and Genes 10
Genetic Diagrams 11
Genetic Diagrams and Disorders 13
Mixed Questions — B1 Topic 1 15

B1 Topic 2 — Responding to Change

Homeostasis 17
Hormones and Nerves 18
The Nervous System 19
Investigating Stimuli and Reflexes 21
Insulin and Diabetes 23
Plant Growth Hormones 25
Plant Growth Hormones — Experiments 26
Commercial Use of Plant Hormones 27
Mixed Questions — B1 Topic 2 28

B1 Topic 3 — Inter-relationships

Drugs 30
Smoking, Alcohol and Organ Transplants 32
Infectious Diseases 34
More About Drugs 36
Antiseptics and Antibiotics 37
Energy and Biomass 39
Parasitism and Mutualism 41
Human Activity and the Environment 42
Recycling 44
Indicator Species 45
The Carbon Cycle 46
The Nitrogen Cycle 48
Mixed Questions — B1 Topic 3 49

C1a Topic 1 — The Earth's Sea and Atmosphere

The Evolution of the Atmosphere 53
Today's Atmosphere 55

C1a Topic 2 — Materials from the Earth

The Three Different Types of Rock 56
Using Limestone 58
Limestone and Thermal Decomposition 61
Atoms and Mass in Chemical Reactions 63
Balancing Equations 64
Mixed Questions — C1a Topics 1 & 2 66

C1b Topic 3 — Acids

Hazard Symbols 69
Acids and Alkalis 70
Hydrochloric Acid and Indigestion Tablets 71
Reactions of Acids 72
Electrolysis 76

C1B TOPIC 4 — OBTAINING AND USING METALS

Metal Ores 78
Reduction of Metal Ores 79
Properties of Metals 81
Making Metals More Useful 83
Recycling 85

C1B TOPIC 5 — FUELS

Fractional Distillation of Crude Oil 86
Burning Fuels 88
Environmental Problems 89
More Environmental Problems 90
Biofuels 92
Fuel Cells 94
Measuring the Energy Content of Fuels 95
Alkanes and Alkenes 96
Cracking Hydrocarbons 97
Using Alkenes to Make Polymers 98
Mixed Questions — C1b Topics 3, 4 & 5 100

P1A TOPIC 1 — VISIBLE LIGHT AND THE SOLAR SYSTEM

Changing Ideas About the Solar System 105
Waves — Basic Principles 107
Reflection and Refraction 109
Lenses 110
Simple and Reflecting Telescopes 112

P1A TOPIC 2 — THE ELECTROMAGNETIC SPECTRUM

Electromagnetic Waves 113
The Dangers of Electromagnetic Radiation 115
Radio Waves and Microwaves 116
Infrared Radiation 117
Visible Light, UV and X-rays 118
Gamma Rays and Ionising Radiation 120

P1A TOPIC 3 — WAVES AND THE UNIVERSE

The Solar System 121
Is Anybody Out There? 122
Looking Into Space 123
Space and Spectrometry 124
The Life Cycle of Stars 125
The Origins of the Universe 126
Mixed Questions — P1a Topics 1, 2 & 3 128

P1B TOPIC 4 — WAVES AND THE EARTH

Ultrasound and Infrasound 132
The Earth's Structure 134
Seismic Waves 135

P1B TOPIC 5 — GENERATION & TRANSMISSION OF ELECTRICITY

Electric Current and Power 137
Generating Electricity 139
Non-Renewable Energy and Power Stations 141
Using Renewable Energy Resources (1) 142
Using Renewable Energy Resources (2) 143
Comparison of Energy Resources 144
Electricity and the National Grid 146
Energy Efficiency & Cost-Efficiency 148

P1B TOPIC 6 — ENERGY AND THE FUTURE

Energy Transfer 150
Energy Transformations 151
Heat Radiation 152
Mixed Questions — P1b Topics 4, 5 & 6 154

Published by CGP

From original material by Paddy Gannon.

Editors:
Charlotte Burrows, Katherine Craig, Ben Fletcher, Helena Hayes, Felicity Inkpen,
Rosie McCurrie, Edmund Robinson, Jane Sawers, Karen Wells, Sarah Williams.

Contributors:
Steve Coggins, Max Fishel, Dr Iona MJ Hamilton, Rebecca Harvey, Frederick Langridge,
Andy Rankin, Claire Ruthven, Adrian Schmit, Sidney Stringer Community School,
Pat Szczesniak, Paul Warren.

ISBN: 978 1 84146 721 4

With thanks to Barrie Crowther, Janet Cruse-Sawyer, Catherine Davis, Mary Falkner,
Hayley Thompson and Dawn Wright for the proofreading.
With thanks to Jan Greenway, Laura Jakubowski and Laura Stoney for the copyright research.

Graph on page 35 to show the number of cases of TB in the UK between 1997 and 2005 ©
The United Kingdom Parliament. Parliamentary material is reproduced with the permission
of the Controller of HMSO on behalf of Parliament.

Table of Use of Limestone data on pages 59 and 60 © East Midlands Aggregates Working Party
Annual Report (via National Stone Centre - publisher).

Atmospheric CO_2 graph on page 55 reproduced with kind permission from Earth System
Research Laboratory, National Oceanic and Atmospheric Administration, and Scripps
Institution of Oceanography, University of California.

Graph of global temperature variation on page 90 reproduced with permission of the Climatic
Research Unit, School of Environmental Sciences, University of East Anglia: www.cru.uea.ac.uk.

Every effort has been made to locate copyright holders and obtain permission to reproduce
sources. For those sources where it has been difficult to trace the originator of the work,
we would be grateful for information. If any copyright holder would like us to make an
amendment to the acknowledgements, please notify us and we will gladly update the book
at the next reprint. Thank you.

Groovy website: www.cgpbooks.co.uk

Printed by Elanders Ltd, Newcastle upon Tyne.
Jolly bits of clipart from CorelDRAW®
Based on the classic CGP style created by Richard Parsons.

Classification

Q1 Look at the list of **kingdoms** on the right and answer the questions below.

| Protoctists |
| Prokaryotes |
| Fungi |
| Plants |
| Animals |

a) Circle the kingdom that has no nucleus.

b) Give **one** reason why fungi are not placed in the plant kingdom.

....

c) Name **one** feature that protoctists have in common with prokaryotes.

....

d) Explain why viruses cannot be placed in any of the kingdoms listed above.

....

Q2 Organisms can be **classified** into kingdoms and then smaller groups, e.g. species.

a) Complete the subdivision of kingdoms using the words given below.

kingdom ⟶ phylum ⟶ .... ⟶ .... ⟶ .... ⟶ .... ⟶ species

genus   order   class   family

b) For each of the following organisms, give **two** features that can be useful when classifying them.

i) Plants ....

ii) Animals ....

c) Describe the main characteristic of organisms in the phylum Chordata.

....

Q3 Animals can be classified as **vertebrates** or **invertebrates**. Vertebrates can be placed into one of five **classes** — fish, amphibians, reptiles, birds and mammals.

a) What is the main difference between vertebrates and invertebrates?

....

b) List **three** things that scientists take into account when dividing vertebrates into classes.

1. ....

2. ....

3. ....

c) Explain why some vertebrates, like the **duck-billed platypus**, aren't very easy to classify.

....

....

2

<u>More on Classification</u>

Q1 You are given a **sample** of a plant and an **identification key**.

Use the key to identify the plant **from the sample** shown.

Type of plant:.................................

1.	Does the plant have seeds?	Yes – go to 2.
		No – go to 3.
2.	Does the plant have flowers?	Yes – it is a flowering plant.
		No – go to 4.
3.	Does the plant have long stems with lots of small leaves?	Yes – it is a fern.
		No – go to 5.
4.	Does the plant produce cones?	Yes – it is a conifer.
		No – it is a grass.
5.	Does the plant have tiny leaves?	Yes – it is a moss.
		No – is it a fungus?

Q2 The diagram on the right shows a **group of species** that live in **neighbouring** areas.

a) Which **two** species definitely cannot interbreed?

....

b) What is the name for a group of species like this?

....

Western greenish warbler ■ Two-barred warbler ■

Himalayan mountains

Greenish warbler

Key: ↔ Interbreeds
■—■ Cannot interbreed

Q3 Species are named using the **binomial system**.

a) What exactly does **binomial** mean?

....

b) Give **three** advantages of the binomial classification of organisms.

....

....

Q4 Explain why each of the following facts might make **accurate classification** of a species difficult.

a) Some plants reproduce **asexually**.

....

....

b) Many duck species **interbreed** to produce **fertile** offspring.

....

....

....

Variation

Q1 Complete this passage by circling the **best** word or phrase from each highlighted pair.

> Usually, organisms of the same species **have differences** / **are identical**.
>
> This is partly because different organisms have different **genes** / **cells**, which
>
> they inherit from their parents. **Siblings** / **Identical twins** are exceptions to this.
>
> But even these usually have some different features, such as **hair style** / **eye colour**,
>
> and that is due to their **diet** / **environment**. The differences between individual
>
> organisms are known as **variation** / **inheritance**.

Q2 For each of these characteristics, say whether it depends on **genes**, the **environment** or **both**.

a) A person's blood group. ....

b) Someone being able to roll their tongue. ....

c) Someone having cystic fibrosis. ....

d) Someone knowing how to speak Spanish. ....

e) The colour of a plant's flowers. ....

f) The height of a plant. ....

Q3 Helen and Stephanie are identical twins. Helen has dark hair and Stephanie is blonde.

a) Do you think that these are Helen and Stephanie's natural hair colours? Explain your answer.

....

....

b) Helen weighs 7 kg more than Stephanie. Say whether this is due to genes, environment or both, and explain your answer.

....

....

c) Stephanie has a birthmark on her shoulder shaped like a monkey. Helen doesn't.
Do you think birthmarks are caused by your genes? Explain why.

....

....

Top Tips: It's weird to think you only look the way you do because of your genes or your environment, or both. Apart from that dodgy haircut — you've only got yourself to blame for that.

Variation

Q4 Mr O'Riley breeds racehorses. He breeds his best black racing stallion, Snowball, with his best black racing mare, Goldie.

  a) Why is there no guarantee that any foal born will be a champion racer?

  ....

  ....

  b) Will the colour of the newborn foal be due to genes or to environment?

  ....

Q5 Charlie did an experiment to examine the effect of **minerals** on the growth of **two species** of **wheat plant**. He took 60 seedlings of species 1, and divided them into six groups. He repeated this with species 2. He planted each group of seedlings in **identical pots of soil**, but gave them different concentrations of minerals. The table shows the results that Charlie got.

Concentration of mineral / ppm	Change in height of species 1 after 3 weeks / cm	Change in height of species 2 after 3 weeks / cm
0	0	0
100	2	12
200	6	21
300	15	29
400	17	34
500	21	40

  a) Explain why Charlie used **ten** seedlings in each group, instead of just one.

  ....

  b) Charlie put all the seedlings into **identical pots** and used the **same type** of soil.

  i) Explain why he did this.

  ....

  ii) Suggest **two** other things that Charlie should try to keep the same.

  ....

  c) What do Charlie's results suggest about the effect of minerals on the growth of these plants?

  ....

  d) Do you think that the growth of Charlie's plants was affected by genes, the environment or both? Explain your answer.

  ....

  ....

  ....

Continuous and Discontinuous Variation

Q1 State whether there is **continuous** or **discontinuous** variation in each of these characteristics.

a) A person's blood group. ....

b) The distance between a person's pupils. ....

c) The colour of a courgette. ....

d) The height of a sunflower. ....

e) Antibiotic resistance. ....

Q2 Briefly describe a **practical** you could do to show **continuous** variation.

....

....

Q3 Greg measured **two** characteristics in a population of **pea plants**. The results are shown below.

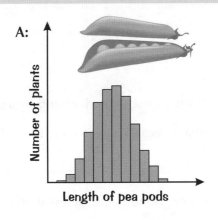

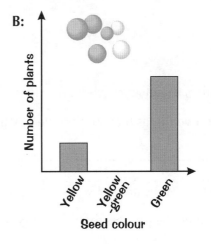

a) i) What does discontinuous variation mean?

....

....

ii) In which characteristic did Greg observe discontinuous variation? ....

b) i) What does continuous variation mean?

....

....

ii) In which characteristic did Greg observe continuous variation? ....

c) Which graph shows the shape of a normal distribution? ....

6

<u>Extreme Environments</u>

Q1 The picture below shows an **angler fish**. Angler fish live in very **deep seas**, where sunlight cannot penetrate.

Luminous organ that
glows in the dark

Huge mouth with
sharp teeth

a) What conditions make the deep sea a hostile environment?

....

....

b) Suggest how the luminous organ on its head helps the angler fish to stay alive in its environment.

....

c) Suggest how a huge mouth can help deep sea fish to stay alive in their environment.

....

Q2 There is usually a much higher density of life found on the seabed around **hydrothermal vents**.

a) Give **two** things that are provided by the vents that make it easier for life to exist around them.

....

b) The food webs around vents are not based on photosynthesis, unlike most others on Earth.

i) Name the process that hydrothermal vent food webs rely on.

....

ii) Briefly explain how this process works.

....

....

....

c) Name the type of organism found at the bottom of hydrothermal vent food webs.

....

Extreme Environments

Q3   Pictures of a **polar bear** and a small rodent called a **kangaroo rat** are shown below.

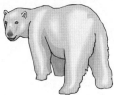   Diagrams are
not to scale.

a)   Which of these animals do you think has the smallest body surface area? ....

b)   Which animal has the smallest body
surface area **compared to its volume**? ....

Remember, long, thin shapes have a big
surface area <u>compared to their volume</u>.

c)   Explain how this animal's **shape** helps to reduce its body surface area compared to its volume.

....

d)   Does having a **smaller** body surface area compared to volume mean that more or less **heat** can be
lost from an animal's body?

....

e)   The polar bear lives in the arctic. It has a **thick layer of blubber**, **large feet** and **greasy fur**.
Explain how each of these adaptations helps the polar bear to survive.

....

....

....

....

Q4   Penguins living in the **Antarctic** have to survive very low temperatures. They have feathers, which
trap air to form an **insulating layer**, and a thick layer of **fat** under their skin. The only places on
their bodies that do not have a thick insulating layer are the feet and the flippers.

a)   The muscles that operate a penguin's feet and flippers are not actually in these parts of its body,
but in the main part of the body. Explain why this is important.

....

....

b)   Penguins sometimes stand very close together in a group. Suggest how this behaviour might help
them to survive.

....

Top Tips: Extreme environments are places with conditions that few species can cope with.
For those that can, life's no picnic but on the plus side there's very little competition from other species.

Natural Selection and Evidence for Evolution

Q1   Explain what is meant by the term **'evolution'**.

....

....

Q2   The theory of evolution has been supported by **evidence** from **DNA research**.
Circle the correct word from the highlighted pair to complete the paragraph below.

> Evolution suggests that all organisms have evolved from shared **common** / **distant** ancestors.
>
> Closely related species diverged (evolved to become different species)
>
> **more recently** / **a long time ago**. Evolution is caused by **rapid** / **gradual** changes in DNA.
>
> Organisms that diverged away from each other recently should have **more** / **less** similar DNA.
>
> Scientists have found that humans and chimps have **similar** / **different** DNA.

Q3   The theory of evolution by **natural selection** was developed by Charles Darwin.
Tick the sentences below that describe aspects of natural selection correctly.

☐   Genes don't vary enough within populations to make individuals look different.

☐   The best adapted animals and plants are most likely to survive.

☐   Some characteristics are passed on through reproduction from parent to offspring.

☐   Over time, there will be a higher proportion of individuals with poorly adapted characteristics compared to those with beneficial characteristics.

☐   Most organisms give birth to less young than can survive to adulthood.

☐   Individuals less well adapted to their environment are less likely to survive and reproduce.

☐   Populations increase rapidly in size, so organisms don't compete.

Q4   Explain how the emergence of **warfarin-resistant rats** supports the theory of evolution by natural selection.

....

....

....

Natural Selection and Evidence for Evolution

Q5 Describe **two** ways in which scientists validate new evidence.

1. ....

....

....

2. ....

....

....

Q6 The **peppered moth** is an insect that is often found on tree bark and is preyed on by birds.
There are **two varieties** of peppered moth — a light form and a dark form.
Until the 1850s, the **light form** was more common, but then the **dark form**
became more widespread, particularly near cities.

Moths on tree bark in unpolluted area   **Moths on tree bark in polluted area**

a) Why do you think the lighter variety of the peppered moth was more common originally?

....   Hint: Use
                                                                                                       the diagrams
....   to help you.

b) In the 1850s, the Industrial Revolution began — there was rapid growth in heavy industries
in Britain. Why do you think the number of dark moths increased after this time?

....

....

c) Do you think a difference in genes or in environment would cause
a dark moth to suddenly appear in a population of light moths? ....

Top Tips: Remember, evolution is a very gradual process — it doesn't just happen overnight.
Make sure you really understand natural selection, so you can apply your knowledge to any question.

Speciation and Genes

Q1 Complete the passage using some of the words given below.

DNA	nucleus	genes	chromosomes	membrane	allele

Most cells in your body contain a structure called the ....

This structure contains strands of genetic information, packaged into ....

These strands are made of a chemical called ....

Sections of genetic material that control different characteristics are called ....

Q2 Write out these structures in order of size, **starting with the smallest**.

nucleus   gene   chromosome   cell

1. .... 2. .... 3. .... 4. ....

Q3 a) Which of the following is the correct definition of the term '**alleles**'? Underline your choice.

'Alleles' is the collective term for all the genes found on a pair of chromosomes.

'Alleles' are different forms of the same gene.

'Alleles' are identical organisms produced by asexual reproduction.

b) Look at the two statements below and circle the one that is **true**.

Alleles give different versions
of a characteristic.

All alleles give identical versions
of a characteristic.

Q4 Isolation and natural selection can lead to **speciation**.

a) What is meant by the term '**isolation**'?

....

b) The diagrams below show the stages of speciation.
Draw lines to match the labels to the correct diagrams.

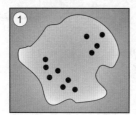 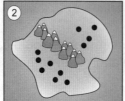 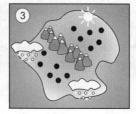 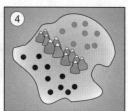

A new species develops.	The populations adapt to new environments.	There are two populations of the same species.	Physical barriers separate the populations.

Genetic Diagrams

Q1   Match each of the terms below with its meaning.

dominant	having two different alleles for a gene
genotype	having two identical alleles for a gene
heterozygous	shown in organisms heterozygous for that trait
homozygous	not shown in organisms heterozygous for that trait
phenotype	the actual characteristics of an individual
recessive	the alleles that an individual contains

Q2   Wilma carries a **recessive** allele for **red** hair and a **dominant** allele for **brown** hair.

a)   What is Wilma's natural hair colour?

....

b)   Is Wilma homozygous or heterozygous for this characteristic?

....

Q3   Fruit flies usually have **red** eyes. However, there are a small number of white-eyed fruit flies. Having **white** eyes is a **recessive** characteristic.

a)   Complete the following sentences with either '**red eyes**' or '**white eyes**'.

i) R is the allele for ....

ii) r is the allele for ....

iii) Fruit flies with alleles **RR** or **Rr** will have ....

iv) Fruit flies with the alleles **rr** will have ....

b)   Two fruit flies have the alleles **Rr**. They fall in love and get it on.

i)   Complete this genetic diagram to show the possible offspring. One's been done for you.

parent's alleles

	R	r
R	RR	
r		

parent's alleles

Read down and across to work out what combination of alleles should be in each box.

ii) What is the probability that the fruit flies' offspring will have **white eyes**?

....

iii) The fruit flies have 16 offspring. How many of the offspring are **likely** to have **red eyes**?

....

Genetic Diagrams

Q4 The **seeds** of pea plants can be **smooth** or **wrinkled**. The allele for smooth seeds (**S**) is dominant. The allele for wrinkled seeds (**s**) is recessive.

a) Complete the genetic diagram below. It shows a cross between a homozygous smooth seed pea plant (genotype **SS**) and a homozygous wrinkled seed pea plant (genotype **ss**).

Parents' alleles:

Gametes' alleles:

Possible combinations of alleles in offspring:

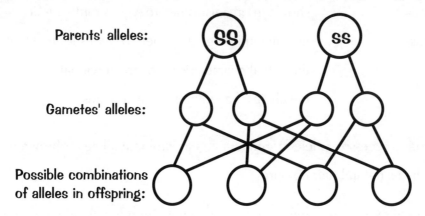

b) In this cross, what is the probability that any one of the offspring will have wrinkled seeds? Tick the correct box.

☐ 100% chance of being wrinkled.

☐ 50% chance of being wrinkled.

☐ 25% chance of being wrinkled.

☐ 0% chance of being wrinkled.

Pictures of peas are very dull.
So here's a picture of a tapir instead.

c) Complete the genetic diagram below to show the possible combinations of alleles in the offspring.

parent's alleles

		S	s
parent's alleles	S		
	s		

d) Mrs Maguire crosses two pea plants with the alleles Ss. Is the following statement **true** or **false**? Tick the correct box.

"If Mrs Maguire gets 12 new seedlings as a result of her cross, the most likely number of seedlings with wrinkled seeds will be 3."

True   False
☐   ☐

Top Tip: Lots of people prefer the grid-type genetic diagrams, but don't be scared of the ones with the blobs and lines. They look like a crazy mess at first but they're actually dead simple — every one of the four offspring circles must have **one letter** from **each** parent, **never** two from the same parent.

Genetic Diagrams and Disorders

Q1   **Sickle-cell anaemia** is a **recessive genetic disorder** which affects the **red blood cells**. The recessive allele for sickle-cell anaemia is **a**, and the dominant allele is **A**.

a) Give **two symptoms** of sickle-cell anaemia.

1. ....   2. ....

b) What combination of alleles is possessed by:

i) a carrier for sickle-cell anaemia.   ....

ii) a sufferer of sickle-cell anaemia.   ....

iii) an unaffected person (who is not a carrier).   ....

Q2   a)   What is cystic fibrosis? Choose from the words below to fill in the gaps.

allele	carrier	genetic	parents	lung	recessive	pancreas	mucus	breathing

Cystic fibrosis is a .... disorder. It is inherited from the .... The disease is .... That means a person must have two copies of the faulty ....
Cystic fibrosis results in the body producing a lot of thick, sticky .... in the air passages, gut and .... Symptoms include difficulty .... and .... infections. A person with one copy of the recessive allele is a ....

b) Complete the following genetic diagram showing the inheritance of cystic fibrosis.

Parents: **Ff**   **Ff**

Gametes:

Offspring:

c) i) In the above genetic diagram, what would be the expected **ratio** of children without cystic fibrosis : children with cystic fibrosis?

....

ii) In the above genetic diagram, what is the probability of a child being a **carrier** of the cystic fibrosis allele (but not having the disease)?

....

Genetic Diagrams and Disorders

Q3 The family tree below shows a family with a history of **cystic fibrosis**. Both Libby and Anne are pregnant. They know the sexes of their babies but not whether they have the disorder.

Karl — Susan

Billy — Anne   Malcolm   Drew — Libby

Baby ?   Baby ?   Ben

Key
- ☐ Male
- ○ Female
- ◧ ◑ Carrier
- ■ ● Sufferer

a) Explain how you can tell from the family tree that the allele for cystic fibrosis is **not** dominant.

....

....

....

....

b) **i)** Complete the table to show the percentage chances of Libby's and Anne's babies being carriers and sufferers.

Sketch a genetic diagram if it helps.

	Carrier	Sufferer
Libby		
Anne		

ii) From the information in part **i)** which mother, Libby or Anne, might decide to have their baby screened for cystic fibrosis?

....

Q4 The **genetic pedigree diagram** below shows the inheritance of **sickle cell anaemia** in one family.

Emma — Ian

James — Martha

Mike   Julian

Key
- ☐ Unaffected male
- ○ Unaffected female
- ■ Male with sickle cell anaemia
- ● Female with sickle cell anaemia

a) Name one female who is **homozygous** for the sickle cell anaemia allele. ....

b) Name one female who is a **carrier** for sickle cell anaemia. ....

c) If James and Martha have another child, what is the chance it will have sickle cell anaemia?

....

Write the genotypes you know on the diagram — this'll help you to work out the ones you don't know.

Top Tip: Pedigree diagrams aren't as scary as they look, just work through them slowly. And remember — with recessive disorders affected individuals are always homozygous, so any children they have will always have at least one recessive allele.

Mixed Questions — B1 Topic 1

Q1   Two types of **goose** found in the UK are the greylag goose and the white-fronted goose.
The Latin name for the greylag goose is *Anser anser* and the white-fronted goose is *Anser albifrons*.

a)   How can you tell that these two geese are different species?

....

b)   How can you tell that the two species must be closely related?

....

c)   What name is given to the system of identifying species by giving them two names?

....

d)   Give a definition for the term '**species**'.

....

e) i)   What **kingdom** do geese belong to?

....

ii)   Give one feature of this kingdom.

....

Q2   The **Arctic fox** is adapted for Arctic conditions.
For example, it has thick white fur.

a)   Explain why thick white fur is useful in Arctic conditions.

....

....

b)   Briefly explain how **natural selection** has led to adaptations such as
these becoming widespread in the Arctic fox population.

....

....

....

c)   A different species of fox moves to the Arctic. Suggest what effect this may have on
the population of Arctic foxes currently living there, and explain why.

....

....

Mixed Questions — B1 Topic 1

Q3 In the Galapagos Islands, different varieties of **giant tortoise** are found on different islands. For example, where the main available food is grass, the tortoises have a dome-shaped shell. However, where the main food is tall cacti, the tortoises have a saddle-backed shell, which allows them to raise their heads higher to feed.

dome-shelled tortoise  saddle-back tortoise

a) Give one example of how the tortoises vary.

....

b) Other than the environment, what causes variation?

....

c) Explain how variation within a species can make accurate classification difficult.

....

d) Different tortoises weigh different amounts.

　i) Is the weight of a tortoise affected by its environment? Explain your answer.

　...

　...

　ii) Is weight an example of continuous or discontinuous variation? Explain your answer.

　...

　...

Q4 Mr and Mrs Carlton are both carriers of **cystic fibrosis** (CF), a **recessive** genetic disorder. The symbol '**c**' is used to represent the recessive allele.

a) What is an allele?

....

....

male gametes　　　female gametes

b) Mr and Mrs Carlton are planning a family. Complete the genetic diagram to show the probability of one of their children suffering from the disorder. Use the symbols **C** and **c** to represent the alleles.

c) What is the probability of the child being a CF sufferer? ....

Homeostasis

Q1 **Homeostasis** is an important process in the human body.

a) Define **homeostasis**.

....

b) Give **two** examples of conditions in the body that are controlled by homeostasis.

1. .... 2. ....

Q2 Complete the following passage by choosing the correct words from those provided.

cold	hairs	nerve	erector	air	warm	fat	muscle

Your skin has lots of .... endings in it that act as temperature receptors.

When they detect that you are too ...., the .... muscles

in the dermis contract. This makes the .... on your skin stand on end.

They trap an insulating layer of ...., which keeps you warm.

Q3 Tim goes outside on a hot day. The sentences below explain how **negative feedback** acts to keep his body temperature constant. Number the sentences to show the correct order.

☐ His brain detects an increase in body temperature.

☐ Tim's body temperature drops to a normal level.

1 Tim's body temperature begins to rise.

☐ It triggers a series of responses that make Tim's body temperature fall.

The first one has been done for you.

Q4 Your body has various techniques for adjusting body temperature to keep it constant.

a) Name the part of the brain that controls body temperature. ....

b) Explain how **sweating** helps to lower your body temperature.

....

....

c) i) Explain what vasodilation and vasoconstriction are.

....

....

ii) How do vasodilation and vasoconstriction help to keep your body temperature constant?

....

....

Hormones and Nerves

Q1 Complete the following passage by choosing the correct words from those given.

blood   fast   long   target   short   chemicals   air   slow   endocrine   impulses   nerve

Hormones are .... which are made in .... glands

and released into the .... They are carried around the body until they

reach a .... organ where they act. Hormones are generally quite

.... to act, but their effects last a .... time.

Q2 Give two differences between responses due to **hormones** and those due to the **nervous system**.

1. ....

2. ....

Q3 Hormones can reach **every cell** in the body. Explain why only the **target cells** respond to the hormone while the others are unaffected.

....

....

Q4 **Neurones** transmit electrical impulses around the body. A diagram of a neurone is shown below.

a) Match the labels to the parts of the neurone by putting the correct letters in the boxes.

A synapse   B nucleus   D axon

C myelin sheath   E dendrons

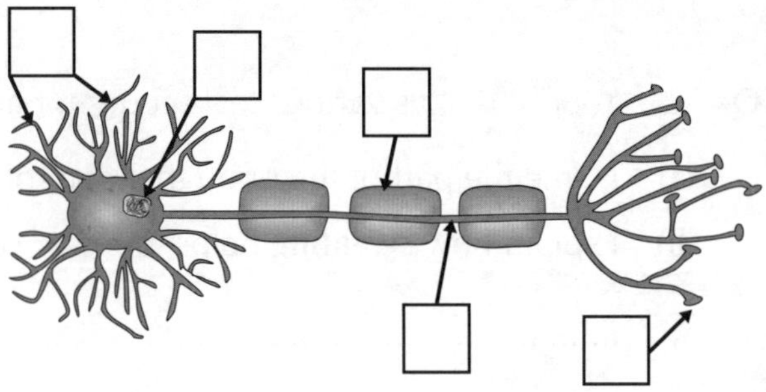

b) Briefly explain the function of:

i) the **dendrons** ....

ii) the **myelin sheath** ....

....

c) Describe the role of **neurotransmitters** in transmitting a nerve impulse.

....

....

The Nervous System

Q1 Decide whether the following statements are **true** or **false**.

True   False

a) Muscles and glands are both effectors.

b) Muscles contract in response to electrical signals.

c) Glands secrete substances in response to a nervous impulse.

d) Hormones are secreted by nerves.

Q2 Complete the following passage by choosing the correct words from the box.

brain	central	motor	effectors	spinal	electrical	sensory

The …….…….......……… nervous system refers to all neurones found in the …….…............….…

and …….….........…… cord. Neurones transmit …….….........…….… impulses from sense

organs to the CNS along …….….........…….… neurones. Impulses from the CNS are sent along

…….….........…….… neurones to …….….........….… .

Q3 Circle the correct word(s) from each pair to complete these sentences about **neurones**.

a) Sensory neurones have **long** / **short** dendrons and **long** / **short** axons.

b) Relay neurones have many **long** / **short** dendrons and **long** / **short** axons.
They carry nerve impulses from **sensory** / **motor** neurones to **sensory** / **motor** neurones.

c) Motor neurones have many short dendrons and **many short axons** / **one long axon**.

Q4 Complete the table with the entries given to show the
sense organs and the type of **receptors** they contain.

Ear

Taste

Skin

Smell

Eye

Sense organ	Receptor type
	Light
Nose	
	Sound / balance
Tongue	
	Touch / temperature

The Nervous System

Q5 Give **two** reasons why it is important for animals to be able to **detect changes** in their surroundings.

....

....

Q6 Explain why a man with a **damaged spinal cord** may not be able to feel someone touching his toe.

....

....

....

Q7 The nervous system is made up of several different parts.

a) Draw arrows between the boxes in the diagram to show the flow of information from a stimulus through the nervous system to the response.

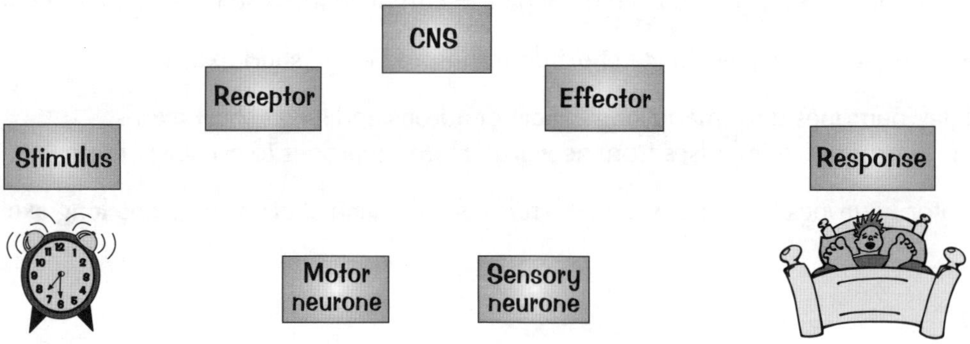

b) Outline the function of the following parts of the nervous system:

i) Receptor cells ....

ii) Sensory neurones ....

iii) CNS ....

iv) Motor neurones ....

v) Effector cells ....

c) The sensory system is driven by stimuli. What is a stimulus?

....

Investigating Stimuli and Reflexes

Q1 Circle the correct answers to complete the following sentences.

a) Reflexes happen more **quickly** / **slowly** than considered responses.

b) The **vertebrae** / **spinal cord** can coordinate a reflex response.

c) The main purpose of a reflex is to **protect** / **display** the body.

d) Reflexes happen **with** / **without** conscious thought.

Q2 When you touch something hot with a finger you **automatically** pull the finger away.
The diagram shows some parts of the nervous system involved in this **reflex action**.

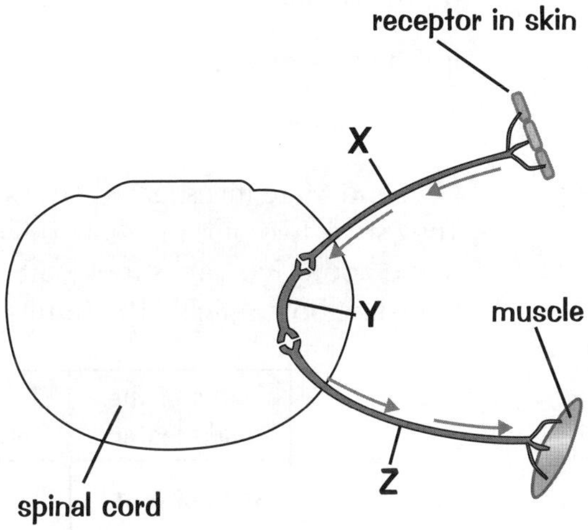

What type of neurone is:

a) neurone **X**? ....

b) neurone **Y**? ....

c) neurone **Z**? ....

receptor in skin

X

Y

muscle

Z

spinal cord

Q3 Explain why a **reflex** reaction is faster than a **voluntary** reaction.

Think about where the
impulse has to go to.

....

....

....

Q4 Explain what a **reflex arc** is.

....

....

....

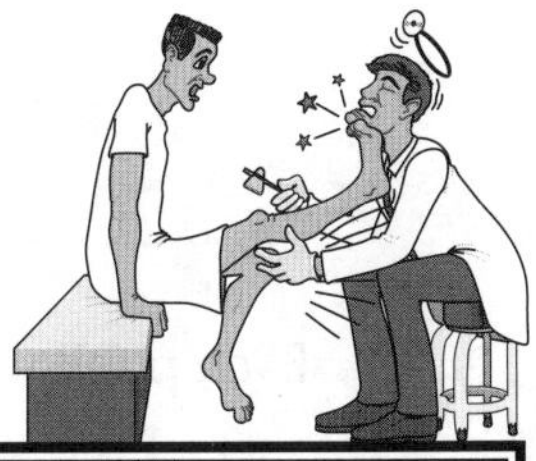

Top Tips: Reflexes are really fast — that's the whole point of them. And the fewer synapses the signals have to cross, the faster the reaction. Doctors test people's reflexes by tapping below their knees to make their legs jerk. This reflex takes less than 50 milliseconds as only one synapse is involved.

Investigating Stimuli and Reflexes

Q5 Read the passage below and then answer the questions.

'Ducking' when an object flies at your head is an example of a reflex action. The eyes detect an object approaching at speed and send a signal to the brain. The brain immediately sends a signal back out to the various muscles that need to contract in order to move the head out of the way.

a) What sort of neurone carries the signal from the eyes to the brain? ....

b) From the passage, identify the following:

i) The stimulus .... **ii)** The receptor ....

iii) The effectors .... **iv)** The response ....

Q6 John and Marc investigated how **sensitive** different parts of the body are to **pressure**. They stuck two pins in a cork 0.5 cm apart. The pins were placed on different parts of the body. Ten pupils took part — they were blindfolded and reported "yes" or "no" to feeling both points. The results of the experiment are shown in the table.

Area of the body tested	Number of pupils reporting 'yes'
Sole of foot	2
Knee	3
Fingertip	10
Back of hand	5
Lip	9

a) Which part of the body do the results suggest is:

i) most sensitive? .... **ii)** least sensitive? ....

b) From the results above, which part of the body do you think contains the greatest concentration of **pressure receptors**? Explain your answer.

....

....

c) John and Marc took it in turns to test the pupils. Their teacher suggested that if only one of the boys had done all the testing, the experiment would have been fairer. Explain why.

....

....

d) Each pupil was tested once. Suggest how you might make the test more reliable.

....

....

Insulin and Diabetes

Q1   Most people's **blood sugar** level is controlled as part of **homeostasis**.

a)   Where does the **sugar** in your blood come from?

....

b)   Name the **two** main **organs** that are involved in the control of blood sugar levels.

....

c)   Name **two hormones** involved in the regulation of blood sugar level.

....

Q2   Complete the flow chart to show what happens when the **glucose** level in the blood gets too **high**.

> Blood contains too much glucose.

> .... is released by the ....

> .... makes the .... store glucose.
> Excess blood glucose is converted to ....

> .... is removed from the ....

> Blood glucose level is now ....
> So .... stops being released.

Q3   Explain how the blood sugar level is controlled when there is **not enough** glucose in the blood.

....

....

....

Insulin and Diabetes

Q4 Approximately **2.6 million** people in the UK have **diabetes**.

a) Explain what **type 1** diabetes is.

....

b) i) Choose the correct word to complete the following sentence:

People with type 1 diabetes can control their blood glucose by injecting insulin into the **subcutaneous fat / pancreas**.

ii) How does taking regular exercise affect the amount of insulin a person needs to inject?

....

c) Explain what **type 2** diabetes is.

....

....

d) Give **two** ways in which type 2 diabetes can be controlled.

1. ....

2. ....

e) What is the link between type 2 diabetes and obesity?

....

Q5 Bob has a height of 1.85 m and a mass of 100 kg.
Jim has a height of 175 cm and a mass of 95 kg.

Make sure you use kg and m in your calculations.

a) Calculate the BMI of:

i) Bob ....

....

ii) Jim ....

....

b) Who would be classified as obese: Jim, Bob, neither or both? Explain your answer.

....

Top Tips: Although diabetes is a serious disease, many diabetics are able to control their blood sugar level and carry on with normal lives. Sir Steve Redgrave even won a gold medal at the Olympics after he had been diagnosed with type 1 diabetes.

Plant Growth Hormones

Q1 Decide whether the following statements are **true** or **false**.

True False

a) Plant shoots grow away from light. ☐ ☐

b) Plant roots grow in the same direction that gravity acts. ☐ ☐

c) If the tip of a shoot is removed, the shoot may stop growing upwards. ☐ ☐

d) Gibberellin affects seed germination and flowering. ☐ ☐

Q2 Some potted plants are growing in a shed lit only by **electric lights**. Circle the letters above the lights that have **broken**.

A   B   C   D   E

Q3 Draw lines to match the two phrases below with their correct **definition** from underneath.

Positive phototropism   Positive gravitropism

Growing towards water | Growing upwards | Growing towards light | Growing downwards

Q4 Choose the correct word from each pair to complete the following paragraph.

When a shoot tip is exposed to light from one side, auxin accumulates on the side that's in the **light / shade**. This makes the cells elongate **faster / slower** on the shaded side, so the shoot bends **away from / towards** the light. In roots, auxin accumulates on the **upper / lower** side. This makes the cells elongate **faster / slower** on the upper side, so the root bends **downwards / upwards**.

Q5 **Auxin** affects plant shoots and roots differently.

a) Describe the **difference** between how auxin affects cells in the shoots and in the roots of plants.

....

....

b) Some side roots of plants grow at an angle to the main root, instead of straight down under the influence of gravity. Suggest why this might be an **advantage** for the plant.

....

Plant Growth Hormones — Experiments

Q1   Some students watered **four seeds** with four **different solutions** for one month. The table below shows their results.

Solution	Plant height (cm)
Water	19
Water + auxin	27
Water + gibberellin	25
Water + auxin + gibberellin	33

a)   Describe what the results show.

....

....

b)   Suggest what the students should do to increase the **reliability** of their results.

....

....

Q2   Vicky used three seedlings to investigate plant growth. Each seedling was prepared differently (see table). All three were placed in the same conditions, exposed to light from **one** direction and left for five hours. She recorded her results in the table below.

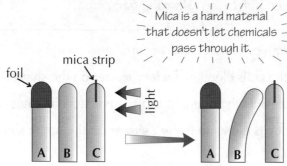

Mica is a hard material that doesn't let chemicals pass through it.

Seedling	Preparation	Observation after 5 hours
A	foil covering tip	no change
B	left alone	tip bent towards the light
C	mica strip through centre of tip	no change

a)   Suggest why seedling A and seedling C failed to respond to the light.

Seedling A ....

....

Seedling C ....

....

b)   Suggest how the experiment could be improved.

....

Commercial Use of Plant Hormones

Q1 Describe four ways in which **plant hormones** can be used **commercially**.

1. ....

2. ....

3. ....

4. ....

Q2 Ronald owns a fruit farm which grows satsumas. The fruit is picked before it is ripe and transported to market.

fruit picked ⟹ fruit packaged ⟹ fruit transported to market ⟹ fruit displayed

a) Suggest why the satsumas are picked before they are ripe.

....

....

b) i) How could the unripened satsumas be ripened in time to reach the market?

....

ii) At what stage in the diagram above should the satsumas be ripened?

....

Q3 Sanjay owns two neighbouring fields — **Field A** and **Field B**. They are an identical size, have the same soil and he uses the same fertiliser regime for both. The only difference is that he applies a weedkiller containing plant growth hormones to Field B but not Field A.

This table shows the yields for both fields.

Year	1997	1998	1999	2000	2001
Barley yield from field A, kg/ha	35	28	33	37	34
Barley yield from field B, kg/ha	48	39	44	49	43

a) What effect did the weedkiller have on crop yield?

....

b) Explain how this type of weedkiller works.

....

....

Mixed Questions — B1 Topic 2

Q1   **Reflex actions** are **automatic responses** to a stimulus.

a)   Give one advantage of reflex actions to the body.

....

b)   Which part of the nervous system is used to coordinate a reflex response?

....

c)   Below are two situations which would cause reflex actions.

A: Stepping on a drawing pin with bare feet.
B: Smelling food when hungry.

Saliva production often increases when you smell food.

Complete the table below for each of the examples given above.

	A	B
stimulus		
receptor		
effector		
response		

Q2   **Hormones** and **neurones** pass signals around the body.

a)   Hormones can affect different parts of the body at the same time. Explain how.

....

....

b)   Are the effects of hormones **long-lasting** or **short-lasting** compared to the effect of nerves?

....

c)   Where nerves are joined together, chemicals transmit the message between them.

i)   What is the name for this **connection** between nerves?

....

ii)   What is the name of the **type of chemical** that transmits messages between nerve endings?

....

d)   Give the name for a pathway of neurones that goes from stimulus to response **without** passing through the conscious part of the brain.

....

Mixed Questions — B1 Topic 2

Q3 The diagram below shows how blood sugar level is controlled in humans.

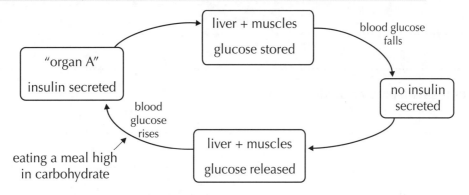

a) Name "organ A" in the diagram above.

....

b) Excess glucose is removed from your blood and stored in the liver and muscles.

i) Which hormone brings about the removal of glucose?

....

ii) Some people have diabetes (type 1) and cannot produce this hormone.
Briefly describe **one** way that diabetes is **controlled**.

....

Q4 A farmer watered 100 poppy plants and 100 wheat plants. He watered 50 of each plant species with a solution containing a **growth hormone**, and the other 50 just with **water**. The results are shown in the table below.

Plant species	Average height without growth hormone	Average height with growth hormone
Poppy (a broad-leaved weed)	65.8 cm	89.2 cm
Wheat (a narrow-leaved crop)	70.3 cm	70.2 cm

a) Describe the results shown in the table.

....

b) Suggest a potential use of large doses of the growth hormone for wheat farmers.

....

c) Name a plant hormone that could produce the results seen in poppies.

....

B1 Topic 3 — Inter-relationships

Drugs

Q1 a) What is a drug?

....

....

b) What does the term physical addiction mean?

....

....

c) Some drugs cause the body to develop a tolerance to them. What does this mean?

....

....

Q2 a) **Complete** the table below, which shows different types of drug and their effects on the body.

Type of drug	Example	Effects
Depressants		
	Morphine	Decrease the feeling of pain
Stimulants		
		Distort what is seen and heard

b) Briefly describe how morphine decreases the feeling of pain.

....

Q3 Different drugs have different effects on the nervous system.

a) Why is it dangerous to drive or operate machinery when under the influence of a depressant?

....

....

b) Caffeine is a legal drug in the UK. Why isn't it dangerous to drive under the influence of this drug?

....

....

<u>Drugs</u>

Q4 Tom and Jane did an experiment on **reaction times**. Tom held a ruler vertically between Jane's thumb and forefinger, with her forefinger in line with the zero mark. Tom dropped the ruler **without warning** and measured how far it fell before Jane caught it. They repeated their experiment three times. The three measurements (**in cm**) were **15**, **28** and **8**.

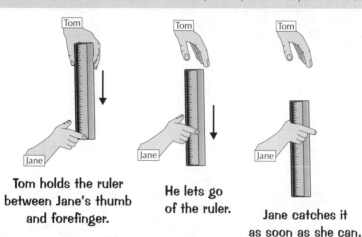

Tom holds the ruler between Jane's thumb and forefinger.

He lets go of the ruler.

Jane catches it as soon as she can.

a) Suggest two reasons why the results varied so much.

1. ....

2. ....

b) Tom and Jane's teacher said that they needed to repeat their experiment at least 10 times. Why did she suggest so many repeats?

....

....

Tom and Jane tested the effect of **caffeine** on reaction times. They each drank one cup of coffee — either **regular** coffee or **decaffeinated** coffee. Then they repeated the above experiment 10 times.

c) Tom and Jane made sure neither of them knew which cup of coffee they had. Why do you think they did this?

....

....

....

d) Their results are shown in the table on the right.

i) Complete the table.

ii) Who do you think drank the regular coffee?

....

Trial	Distance before coffee (cm)		Distance after coffee (cm)	
	Tom	Jane	Tom	Jane
1	16	12	22	15
2	27	17	28	9
3	9	8	15	16
4	14	19	7	12
5	11	24	16	21
6	26	21	9	7
7	29	16	24	12
8	18	19	18	17
9	11	6	16	8
10	19	16	20	14
Mean	18			

Smoking, Alcohol and Organ Transplants

Q1 Alcohol has a number of **short-term effects**. State the effects it has on:

a) A person's behaviour.

....

b) A person's vision.

....

c) A person's reactions.

....

Q2 Complete the passage below by choosing the correct words from those given.

harmless   long-term   cleaning   brain   cirrhosis   death   damage   liver   poisonous   blood

As well as affecting a person straight away, alcohol has .... effects, which means

it affects a person in the future.   Alcohol is .... Normally, the ....

breaks down the toxic alcohol into .... by-products. But drinking too much

too often causes the .... of liver cells, forming scar tissue that starts to block

.... flow through the liver — this is called .... If the liver can't do its

normal job of .... the blood, dangerous substances start to build up and

.... the rest of the body. Too much drinking can also lead to .... damage.

Q3 Smoking tobacco can cause many different **health problems**, including cancer.
However, the habit is still widespread, mainly because smokers find it **difficult to stop**.

a) Explain why people find it difficult to stop smoking.

....

b) Pregnant women are strongly advised not to smoke.
What effect can smoking have on a baby's birth weight?

....

c) Explain how smoking whilst pregnant can cause this problem.

....

....

Top Tips: Tobacco and alcohol are totally legal substances but they're potentially dangerous
drugs too. Alcohol is dangerous if used to excess and cigarettes are just full of poisonous chemicals.

Smoking, Alcohol and Organ Transplants

Q4 Many people wish to **donate organs** after they die so that other people can benefit.

a) What can a person do to officially state their wish to donate their organs?

....

b) Who can **object** to the removal of the donor's organs?

....

c) A patient who had liver cirrhosis after drinking too much alcohol was given a liver transplant.

　i) Give a reason **in support** of this operation.

　..

　ii) Give **one** possible reason why some people would be **against** this operation.

　..

d) What might a clinically obese person be asked to do before being considered for a heart transplant?

....

Q5 The graph shows how the number of **smokers** aged between 35 and 54 in the UK has changed since 1950.

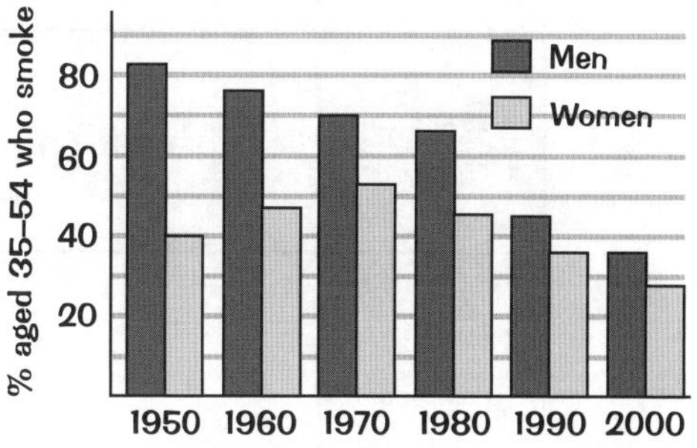

a) What percentage of **men** smoked in 1970?

....

b) Describe the main **trends** you can see in this graph.

....

....

....

c) Why are smokers more likely to suffer from **cancers**?

....

....

Infectious Diseases

Q1 Decide whether the following statements are **true** or **false**.

		True	False
a)	Infectious diseases are caused by pathogens.	☐	☐
b)	Infectious diseases can be passed on genetically.	☐	☐
c)	All pathogens are bacteria.	☐	☐
d)	Living organisms do not cause infectious diseases.	☐	☐

Q2 Complete the following passage by circling the correct words.

Influenza is caused by a **virus / bacterium**. It is spread by **vectors / droplets in air** — in the same way as **colds / Salmonella**. It's transmitted when an infected person coughs or sneezes near someone. People with symptoms should **stay at home / go to work** and use tissues when they sneeze.

HIV is a **virus / bacterium** that causes **Salmonella / AIDS**. It is passed on via **contact / body fluids**.

Q3 Complete the table below about the different ways in which organisms transmit diseases.

Disease	Cholera	Salmonella		Athlete's foot
Type of organism	bacterium			
How it is transmitted			by the *Anopheles* mosquito	

Q4 Dysentery is a disease that is spread by a **vector**.

a) Name a vector that carries dysentery.

....

b) How does this vector spread dysentery?

....

Infectious Diseases

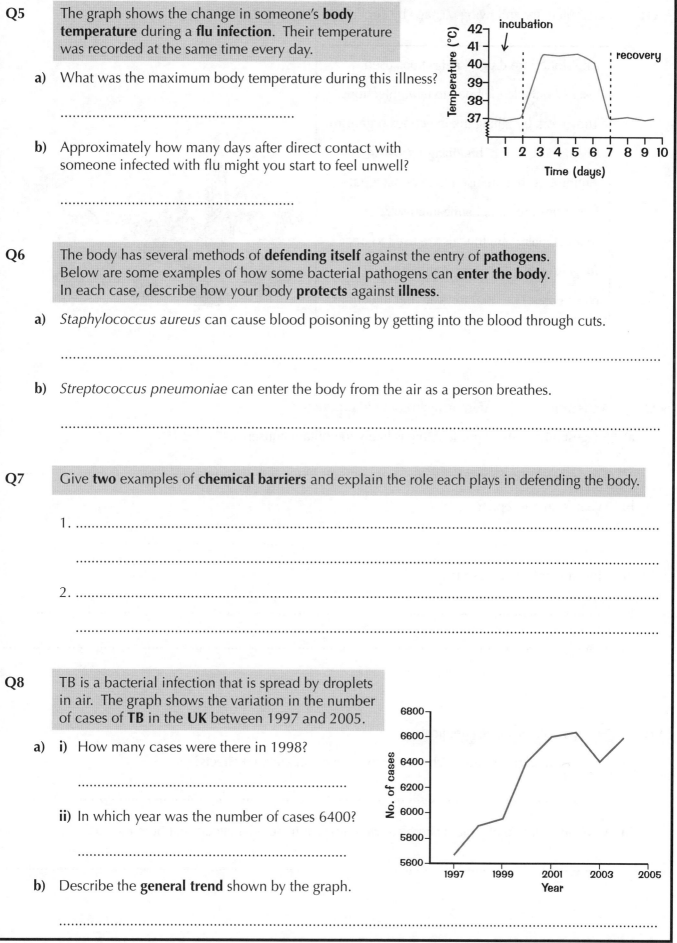

Q5   The graph shows the change in someone's **body temperature** during a **flu infection**. Their temperature was recorded at the same time every day.

a)   What was the maximum body temperature during this illness?

....

b)   Approximately how many days after direct contact with someone infected with flu might you start to feel unwell?

....

Q6   The body has several methods of **defending itself** against the entry of **pathogens**. Below are some examples of how some bacterial pathogens can **enter the body**. In each case, describe how your body **protects** against **illness**.

a)   *Staphylococcus aureus* can cause blood poisoning by getting into the blood through cuts.

....

b)   *Streptococcus pneumoniae* can enter the body from the air as a person breathes.

....

Q7   Give **two** examples of **chemical barriers** and explain the role each plays in defending the body.

1. ....

....

2. ....

....

Q8   TB is a bacterial infection that is spread by droplets in air. The graph shows the variation in the number of cases of **TB** in the **UK** between 1997 and 2005.

a)   i)   How many cases were there in 1998?

....

ii)   In which year was the number of cases 6400?

....

b)   Describe the **general trend** shown by the graph.

....

More About Drugs

Q1 Complete the following passage by circling the correct words.

Antibiotics are **drugs / antiseptics** used
inside / outside the body to treat infections.
They work by killing the infectious organism
or stopping it from **breathing / growing**.
Antibiotics that are used to treat bacterial
infections are called **antibacterials /
probacterials**. Antifungals are used to treat
fungal / viral infections. Antibiotics
can / cannot be used to treat viral infections.

Q2 **Antiseptics** are found in many household products.

a) Suggest a household product that is likely to contain antiseptics.

....

b) What is an antiseptic?

....

c) How are antiseptics used?

....

....

Q3 Some **plants** produce chemicals.

a) Why might plants produce chemicals that have antibacterial effects?

....

b) Give an example of a plant chemical which has antibacterial effects that humans use.

....

Antiseptics and Antibiotics

Q1 The graph shows the number of bacteria in Gary's blood during a two-week course of **antibiotics**.

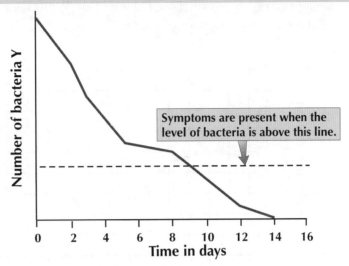

Symptoms are present when the level of bacteria is above this line.

Number of bacteria Y

Time in days

a) Define the term "antibiotic".

....

b) How long after starting the course of antibiotics will Gary's symptoms disappear? ....

c) Why is it important for Gary to **finish** his full course of antibiotics?

....

d) Give an **example** of a strain of bacteria that is resistant to antibiotics.

....

Q2 Jenny went to the doctor because she had **flu**. The doctor advised her to stay in bed for a while but didn't give her any antibiotics.

a) Why wouldn't the doctor give her any antibiotics for her condition?

....

b) Explain how bacteria can develop **resistance** to an antibiotic.

....

....

....

....

Top Tips: Antibiotics are just great but they should be used with care as nobody wants a nasty superbug hanging around, bugging everyone. You need to know how these can develop. So learn it.

Antiseptics and Antibiotics

Q3   In 1960, a **new antibiotic** was discovered which was very effective against **disease X**. Doctors have been prescribing this drug ever since. The graph below shows the number of deaths from disease X over a number of years.

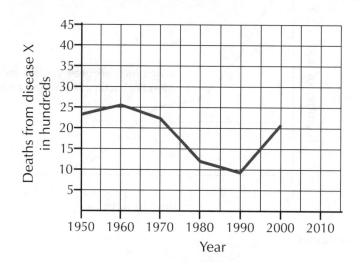

a)   Assuming nothing changes, use the graph to **predict** the number of deaths from disease X in **2010**.

....

b)   Suggest a reason for the **fall** in deaths from the disease between 1960 and 1990.

....

c)   Suggest a reason for the **sudden rise** in deaths from the disease between 1990 and 2000.

....

....

Q4   Gavin and Van carried out an experiment at school to investigate the effectiveness of five different **antiseptics** (1–5). They spread some bacteria onto a sterile agar plate. They then placed discs of filter paper, impregnated with the five different antiseptics, onto the bacterial culture.

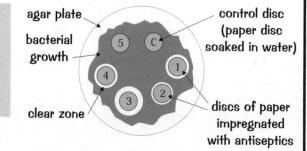

a)   Explain what has happened in the "clear zone" labelled on the diagram.

....

b)   Which of the antiseptics (1–5) was the most effective against these bacteria? ....

Energy and Biomass

Q1   Complete the sentences below by **circling** the most appropriate word each time.

a)   **Plants** / **Animals** can make their own food by a process called **photosynthesis** / **respiration**.

b)   To obtain energy animals must **decay** / **eat** plant material or other animals.

c)   Animals release energy from food through the process of **photosynthesis** / **respiration**.

d)   Some of the energy obtained by animals from their food is **gained** / **lost** before
it reaches organisms at later steps of the food chain. This is mainly because it has been
used for **growth** / **movement**.

Q2   Read the sentences below about **food chains**, **energy transfer**
and **pyramids of biomass**. Then tick the boxes to show
which sentences are true and which are false.

True **False**

a)   Plants convert all the light energy that falls on them into glucose.   ☐ ☐

b)   Energy is used in respiration at each stage in a food chain.   ☐ ☐

c)   Only energy is passed between the steps of food chains.   ☐ ☐

d)   Animals that have to maintain a constant body temperature
lose more energy as heat than animals that don't.   ☐ ☐

e)   Pyramids of biomass always start with a producer.   ☐ ☐

f)   Pyramids of biomass can only have three steps.   ☐ ☐

Q3   A **food chain** is shown below.

leaf it out

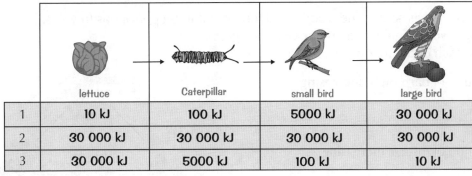

	lettuce	Caterpillar	small bird	large bird
1	10 kJ	100 kJ	5000 kJ	30 000 kJ
2	30 000 kJ	30 000 kJ	30 000 kJ	30 000 kJ
3	30 000 kJ	5000 kJ	100 kJ	10 kJ

a)   Which row, 1, 2 or 3, shows the amount of energy available at each trophic level? ....

b)   Explain your reasoning for part **a)**.

....

Energy and Biomass

Q4 A single **robin** has a mass of 15 g and eats caterpillars. Each robin eats 25 **caterpillars** that each have a mass of 2 g. The caterpillars feed on 10 **stinging nettles** that together have a mass of 500 g. Study the pyramid diagrams shown and then answer the questions that follow.

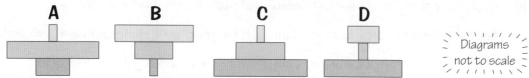

A   **B**   **C**   **D**

Diagrams not to scale

a) Which diagram is most likely to represent a pyramid of biomass for these organisms? ....

b) Explain how you decided on your answer to part **a)** above.

....

....

c) The stinging nettles are the first trophic level. Where does their energy initially come from?

....

d) Explain why food chains rarely have more than five trophic levels.

....

....

Q5 The **food web** below shows how species in a woodland are **interdependent**.

a) What is meant by the term "interdependent"?

....

....

b) Last year a chemical was spilt in the woods, and turned out to be poisonous to voles. The population of **voles** significantly **decreased**. Suggest an explanation for each of the following consequences:

i) The population of barn owls **decreasing**.

....

ii) The population of insects **increasing**.

....

iii) The population of insects **decreasing**.

....

Barn owl

Vole   Insects   Bird

Grass and seeds

Parasitism and Mutualism

Q1 **Parasitism** and **mutualism** are both ways that one species can depend on another species.

a) In a **parasitic relationship** one organism benefits.
What is the name given to the **other** organism in the relationship?

....

b) Put a tick in the box next to the statement that correctly describes **mutualism**.

☐ one organism benefits and the other is neither helped nor harmed

☐ one organism benefits and the other is harmed

☐ both organisms benefit from the relationship

Q2 Draw a line to match each **parasite** with its effect on other organisms.

Mistletoe	Live in the fur and bedding of animals, and feed by sucking their blood.
Tapeworms	Live on human scalps and suck their blood, making them itch.
Fleas	Attach to an animal's intestinal wall and absorb lots of nutrients.
Headlice	Grows on trees and shrubs, absorbing water and nutrients from them.

Q3 The pairs of organisms below have a **mutualistic relationship**.
For each organism state what, if anything, it **gains** from the relationship.

a) oxpeckers ....

buffalo ....

b) nitrogen-fixing bacteria ....

legumes ....

c) chemosynthetic bacteria ....

deep-sea vent tubeworms ....

d) cleaner wrasse (cleaner fish) ....

grouper (larger host fish) ....

Top Tips: An outbreak of headlice is great news for the lice, but bad news for everyone else. This kind of relationship is the same for all parasites — one species thrives while another is harmed.

B1 Topic 3 — Inter-relationships

42

Human Activity and the Environment

Q1 The size of **Earth's population** has an impact on our environment.

a) How would you expect an **increase** in population size to affect the following things?

i) The amount of **raw materials** (including non-renewable energy resources)

....

ii) **Waste disposal**

....

b) Many human activities cause pollution.
Name a **man-made source** of each of the following pollutants:

i) phosphate ....

ii) nitrate ....

iii) sulfur dioxide ....

Q2 The size of the **Earth's population** has changed dramatically in the last 1000 years.

a) Use the table below to plot a graph on the grid, showing how the world's human population has changed over the last 1000 years.

Population size / billions	Year
0.3	1000
0.4	1200
0.4	1400
0.6	1600
1.0	1800
1.7	1900
6.1	2000

b) Circle the correct word to complete each sentence.

i) The size of the Earth's population now is **bigger / smaller** than it was 1000 years ago.

ii) The growth of the population now is **slower / faster** than it was 1000 years ago.

iii) The impact on the environment now is **less / greater** than it was 1000 years ago.

c) Suggest **two** reasons for the sudden increase in the population.

....

....

B1 Topic 3 — Inter-relationships

Human Activity and the Environment

Q3 Rivers and lakes can be **polluted** by **fertilisers** that come from nearby farmland. This often results in the death of many fish.

a) Why are fertilisers essential to modern farming?

....

b) How does the fertiliser get into the rivers and lakes?

....

c) How does pollution by fertilisers cause fish to die?

....

....

....

d) What is the name given to this type of pollution by fertilisers?

....

Q4 A student decided to test the effect of **nitrate fertiliser** on plant growth. She placed **four seeds** into four different Petri dishes. Each dish contained cotton wool soaked in **different concentrations** of nitrate. The results are shown below.

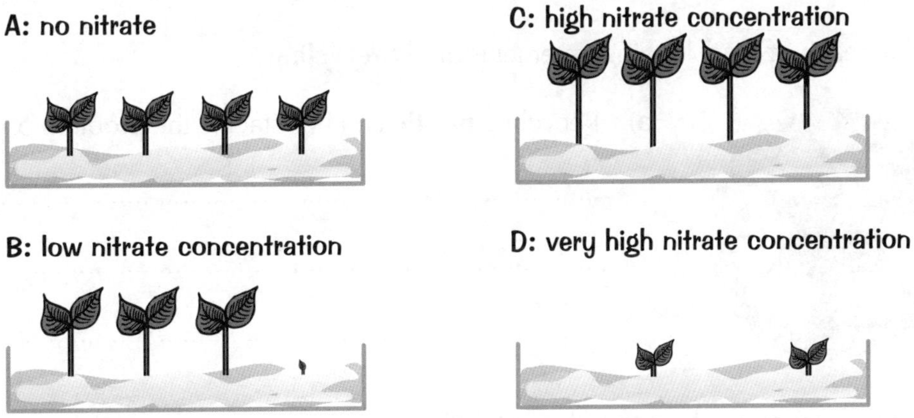

A: no nitrate

C: high nitrate concentration

B: low nitrate concentration

D: very high nitrate concentration

a) Which Petri dish was the control? ....

b) Briefly describe the effects of nitrate fertiliser on plant growth in this experiment.

....

....

....

Recycling

Q1   Tick the boxes to show which of the following are good reasons for **recycling metals**.

☐   The recycling process gives many metals useful new properties.

☐   It uses less energy and therefore less fossil fuel.

☐   The metal produced is purer and so of a higher quality.

☐   Less carbon dioxide is produced as a result.

Q2   There are important **benefits** of recycling, but it is still **not** a perfect solution.

a)   Explain how recycling materials helps to conserve the world's energy resources.

....

....

b)   State three ways in which the recycling process uses energy.

1. ....

2. ....

3. ....

Q3   Explain each of the following statements about **recycling**.

a)   Recycling **plastic** can help tackle the problem of waste disposal.

....

....

....

b)   Recycling **paper** can help to reduce global warming.

Think about the carbon cycle.

....

....

....

Top Tips: The UK isn't great at recycling — we're getting better, but still languishing far behind other European countries. Collection schemes are making things easier, so no more excuses.

Indicator Species

Q1   **Stonefly larvae** and **sludge worms** are often studied to see how much **sewage** is in water.
Juanita took samples of water from where two different drains empty into a river.
She recorded the number of each species in the water samples and her results are shown below.

Site	No. of stonefly larvae	No. of sludge worms
After drain A	22	0
After drain B	0	30

a)   Which drain(s) seem to be polluting the river with sewage?
Circle the correct answer: **Neither Drain / Drain A / Drain B / Drains A and B**

b)   Suggest **two** other indicator species that Juanita could have studied instead.

1. ....   2. ....

Q2   The number of species of **lichen** living in an area can be used as an **indicator** of how
clean the air is there. Scientists did a survey of the number of lichens found on
gravestones at different distances from a city centre. The results are shown below:

Distance from city centre (km)	No. of species found on ten gravestones
0	12
2	13
6	22
16	29
20	30
24	35

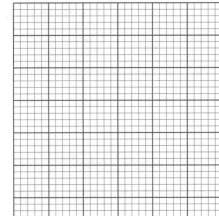

No. of species of lichen

Distance from city centre (km)

a)   Draw a graph of this data on the grid provided.

b)   What **general trend** is shown by the data?

....

....

c)   Give a possible **reason** for this trend.

....

....

d)   Name **another species** that can be used to indicate clean air.

....

The Carbon Cycle

Q1   Complete the diagram below as instructed to show a **part** of the **carbon cycle**.

CO₂ in the air

plant   animal

a)   Add an arrow or arrows labelled **P** to represent **photosynthesis**.

b)   Add an arrow or arrows labelled **R** to represent **respiration**.

c)   Add an arrow or arrows labelled **F** to represent **feeding**.

Q2   Answer the following questions to show how the **stages** in the **carbon cycle** are ordered.

a)   Number the sentences below to show how carbon moves between the air and living things.
The first one has been done for you.

....   Animals eat the plants' carbon compounds.

....**1**....   Carbon dioxide in the air.

....   Plants and animals die.

....   Plants take in carbon dioxide for photosynthesis and make carbon compounds.

b)   Add a point 5 to complete the cycle and show how carbon is returned to the air.

Point 5: ....

Q3   Answer the following questions about the **carbon cycle**.

a)   What is the most common form of carbon found in the atmosphere?

....

b)   What products do plants convert this carbon into?

....

c)   How is the carbon in plants passed on through the food chain?

....

d)   Give **three** things that can happen to dead plants and animals.

1. ....

2. ....

3. ....

The Carbon Cycle

Q4 The diagram below shows one version of the **carbon cycle**.

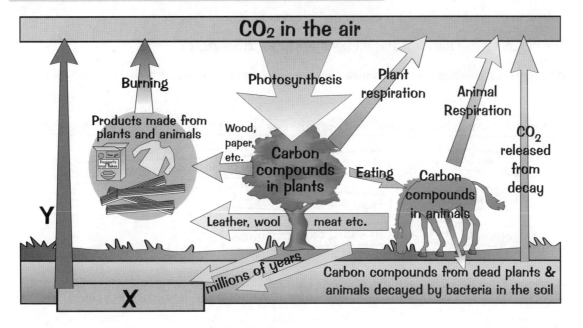

a) Name substance **X** shown on the diagram above. ....

b) Explain why substance **X** contains carbon.

....

....

c) Name the process labelled **Y** on the diagram above. ....

Q5 Nutrients are constantly **recycled**.

a) Name **three** elements (other than carbon) that are recycled in the environment.

....

b) Explain why **microorganisms** are important in recycling nutrients.

....

....

....

Don't just describe what the microorganisms do — explain why it's important.

Top Tips: Lots of substances are **recycled**, not just carbon. They enter organisms when they feed (or photosynthesise) and leave when they die, breathe or poo. That's the great circle of life for you.

The Nitrogen Cycle

Q1 Circle the correct word or phrase to complete the following sentences.

a) Nitrogen is needed to make **protein** / **carbohydrate** / **fat**.

b) The percentage of the air that is nitrogen is **100%** / **21%** / **78%**.

c) Nitrogen is **a reactive** / **an unreactive** gas that **can** / **can't** be used directly by plants and animals.

Q2 Draw lines to match up each type of **organism** below with the way that it obtains **nitrogen**.

Plants

Animals

Bacteria in soil

By breaking down dead organisms and animal waste

From nitrates in the soil

By eating other organisms

Q3 Explain the role of each of the following types of **bacteria** in the **nitrogen cycle**.

a) Decomposer bacteria ....

b) Nitrifying bacteria ....

c) Nitrogen-fixing bacteria ....

Q4 Below is a diagram of the **nitrogen cycle**. Explain what is shown by the arrows labelled:

a) Y ....

....

....

b) Z ....

....

....

c) What role does lightning play in the nitrogen cycle?

....

Q5 A farmer was told that if he planted **legume plants** his soil would be more **fertile**. Explain how the legume plants would increase the fertility of the soil.

....

....

Mixed Questions — B1 Topic 3

Q1   **Malaria** is a disease that is common in tropical areas.

a)   Fill in the blanks in the paragraph using some of the words from the list below.

mosquitoes   guest   agent   old   biting   killed   insecticide

kissing   vector   protozoan   dirty water   lymph   chump

Malaria is a disease caused by a ....   The infection is transmitted from person

to person by ...., which spread the disease by .... people.

An organism which transfers a disease without actually getting it is called a ....

b)   Mosquito coils release smoke that deters mosquitoes.
However, they also contain carcinogens. What is a carcinogen?

....

c)   Quinine is a drug that protects against malaria. In the past it was taken as a tonic mixed with gin, which is an alcoholic drink.

i)   What type of drug is alcohol?

....

ii)   How does this type of drug affect the brain?

....

....

Q2   **Infectious** diseases are diseases which are **transmitted** from one person to another.

a)   What is a pathogen?

....

b)   Name **four** types of pathogen.

....

c)   All pathogens are parasites. What does this mean?

....

d)   How does the respiratory system use physical barriers to stop pathogens from entering the body?

....

....

Mixed Questions — B1 Topic 3

Q3 Human activity causes various types of **air pollution**. Three common air pollutants are:

Carbon dioxide   **Carbon monoxide**   **Sulfur dioxide**

Each statement below refers to one or more of these pollutants.
Indicate which one(s) in the space provided.

a) May be released when fossil fuels are burnt. ....

b) A poisonous gas that prevents red blood cells carrying oxygen. ....

c) Kills blackspot fungi on rose leaves. ....

d) Removed from the air by photosynthesis. ....

Q4 **Legumes** are plants that have nodules on their roots containing **nitrogen-fixing bacteria**.

a) Plants absorb nitrogen compounds from the soil. What is the name of these nitrogen compounds?

....

b) Explain why plants can't get their nitrogen directly from the air.

....

....

c) The legumes and the nitrogen-fixing bacteria have a mutualistic relationship.
Explain fully what this means.

....

....

Q5 **Air pollution** can be measured using both **living** and **non-living indicators**.

a) Explain what each of these methods involve.

....

....

....

b) A sample of **lichens** is taken from trees in two different towns. The sample from **town A** contains 19 organisms of 2 different lichen species. The sample from **town B** contain 36 organisms of 8 different lichen species. Which town do you think is the more polluted? Explain your answer.

....

....

Mixed Questions — B1 Topic 3

Q6 The diagram below shows a **food chain** observed on the savannahs of Tanzania. It also shows the amount of **energy** available in each trophic level.

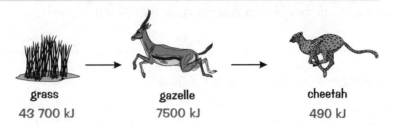

grass   gazelle   cheetah
43 700 kJ   7500 kJ   490 kJ

a) Where does the grass get its energy from?

....

b) Suggest **two** ways in which energy might be lost by the gazelle.

....

....

c) **Carbon** also moves through the food chain. It is continuously being **recycled** from one form to another as the diagram below shows.

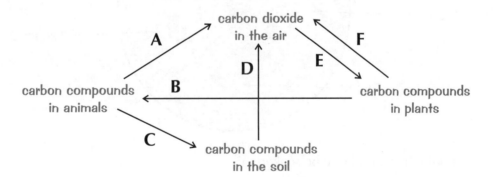

Name the processes labelled **A**, **B**, **C**, **D**, **E** and **F** in the diagram.

A .... B ....

C .... D ....

E .... F ....

d) Also growing on the savannah are Acacia trees which belong to the legume family. They contain bacteria in nodules in their roots, and transfer sugar to the bacteria. The bacteria use this sugar in their respiration. Using this information, add the following arrows and labels to the correct places in the carbon cycle diagram above:

carbon compounds   transfer of sugar   respiration
in bacteria   ⟶   ⟶

Mixed Questions — B1 Topic 3

Q7   **Athlete's foot** is caused by a microorganism that infects the skin.
The disease is treated by applying **antifungal compounds**.

a)   State the type of microorganism that causes athlete's foot.

....

b)   Explain how the microorganism is transmitted.

....

....

c)   The diagram below shows the results of an experiment to test extracts from different plants
for their potential **antifungal properties**. Discs containing different plant extracts dissolved
in ethanol were put onto a Petri dish that had been evenly spread with microbes.
The microbes were allowed to grow.

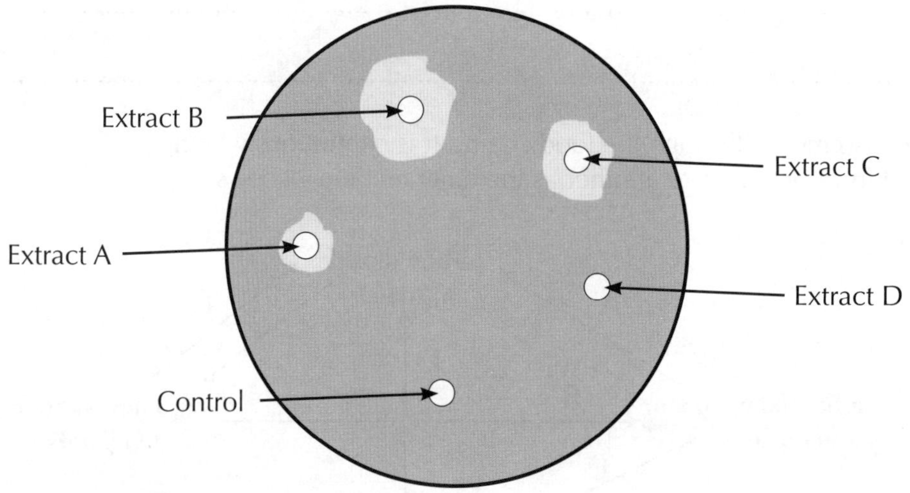

i)   What should the control disc be soaked in?

....

ii) Which extract was the **most** effective?

....

iii) Which extract was the **least** effective?

....

iv) Give **three** variables that should be controlled in this experiment.

1. ....

2. ....

3. ....

The Evolution of the Atmosphere

Q1 Tick the boxes next to the sentences below that are **true**.

When the Earth was formed, its surface was molten. ☐

The Earth's early atmosphere is thought to have been mostly oxygen. ☐

When oxygen started building up in the atmosphere, all organisms began to thrive. ☐

When marine organisms died and were buried under layers of sediment,
the carbon inside them became locked up in carbonate rocks. ☐

Q2 The amount of **carbon dioxide** in the atmosphere has changed over the last 4.5 billion or so years.

Describe how the level of carbon dioxide has changed and explain why this change happened.

....

....

....

....

Q3 Draw lines to put the statements in the **right order** on the timeline. One is done for you.

Present

NOT TO
SCALE

4500 million years ago

*Don't get confused — 4500
million is the same as 4.5 billion.*

The Earth cools down slightly. A thin crust
forms. There's lots of volcanic activity.

Water vapour condenses to form oceans.

The Earth's surface is molten — it's so hot that
any atmosphere just 'boils away' into space.

Green plants evolve over most of the Earth.
They're quite happy in the CO_2 atmosphere.
A lot of the CO_2 dissolves into the oceans.
The green plants also absorb some of the CO_2
and produce O_2 by photosynthesis.

The atmosphere is about four-fifths
nitrogen and one-fifth oxygen.

The build-up of oxygen in the atmosphere allows
more complex organisms to evolve and flourish.
The oxygen also creates the ozone layer.

The Evolution of the Atmosphere

Q4 The pie chart below shows the proportions of the different gases in the Earth's atmosphere today.

a) Add the labels 'Nitrogen', 'Oxygen', and 'Carbon dioxide and other gases'.

Earth's Atmosphere Today

Water vapour

b) Give the approximate percentages of the following gases in the air today:

Nitrogen ....

Oxygen ....

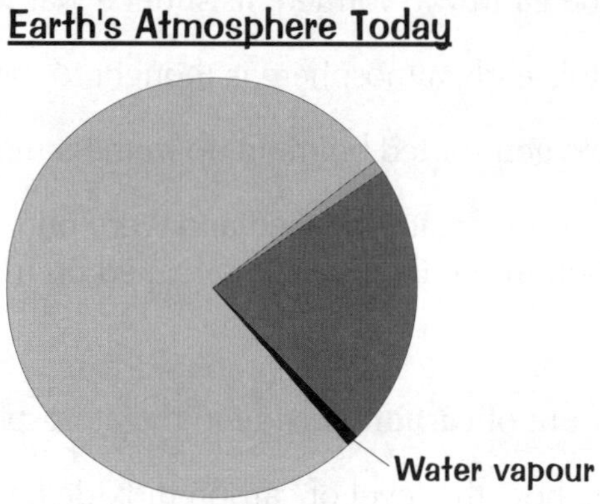

c) This pie chart shows the proportions of different gases that we think were in the Earth's atmosphere 4500 million years ago.

Earth's Atmosphere 4500 Million Years Ago

Carbon dioxide

Nitrogen

Other gases

Water vapour

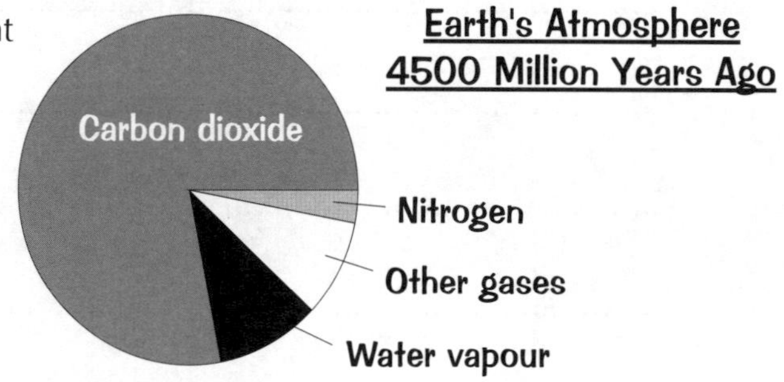

Describe the main differences between today's atmosphere and the atmosphere 4500 million years ago.

....

....

d) Explain why the amount of water vapour has decreased.

....

....

What did the water vapour change into?

e) Explain how the amount of oxygen in the atmosphere increased.

....

f) What were two effects of the rising oxygen levels in the atmosphere?

1. ....

....

2. ....

....

Today's Atmosphere

Q1 The graphs below show the changes in the atmospheric carbon dioxide level and temperature since 1850.

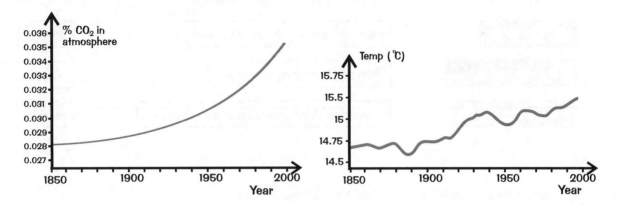

a) i) Name a human activity thought to have contributed to the rise in carbon dioxide over the last 150 years.

....

ii) Describe how this activity is affecting the carbon dioxide level.

....

....

b) Look at the temperature graph.
Has the temperature increased or decreased as the percentage of carbon dioxide has risen?

....

c) The proportion of gases in the atmosphere has changed over millions of years.
Why is it difficult to be precise about the evolution of the atmosphere?

....

Q2 The proportion of oxygen in the atmosphere can be found by heating an excess of copper so that it reacts with oxygen in the air to form copper oxide.

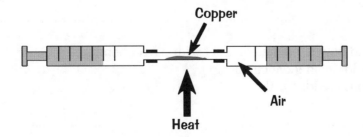

If you started with 50 cm³ of air in the apparatus, how much gas would you end up with?

....

The Three Different Types of Rock

Q1 Join up each **rock type** with the correct **method of formation** and an **example**.

ROCK TYPE   METHOD OF FORMATION   EXAMPLE

igneous rocks	formed from layers of sediment	granite
metamorphic rocks	formed when magma cools	limestone
sedimentary rocks	formed under intense heat and pressure	marble

Q2 Circle the correct words to complete the passage below.

> Igneous rock is formed when magma pushes up into (or through)
>
> the **crust / mantle** and cools.
>
> If the magma cools before it reaches the surface it will **cool slowly / quickly**, forming
>
> **big / small** crystals. This rock is known as **extrusive / intrusive** igneous rock.
>
> However the magma that reaches the surface will cool **slowly / quickly**, forming
>
> **big / small** crystals. This rock is known as **extrusive / intrusive** igneous rock.

Q3 Erica notices that the stonework of her local church contains tiny fragments of **sea shells**.

  a) Suggest an explanation for this.

  ....

  ....

  b) Describe how sedimentary rock is 'cemented' together.

  ....

  ....

  c) Powdered limestone and powdered marble react with other chemicals, such as hydrochloric acid, in an identical fashion. Explain why the reactions are identical.

  Hint: marble is formed from limestone.

  ....

Top Tips: You might think that rocks are just boring lumps of.... rock. But you'd be wrong — rocks are actually boring lumps of different kinds of rock. And the kind of rock they are depends on how they're formed — and this is the stuff you need to make sure you know.

The Three Different Types of Rock

Q4 The diagram below shows the formation of **metamorphic rock.**

a) Add the following labels to the diagram:

Intense heat from below

Metamorphic rock forming here

Pressure from rocks above

Possible uplift to the surface

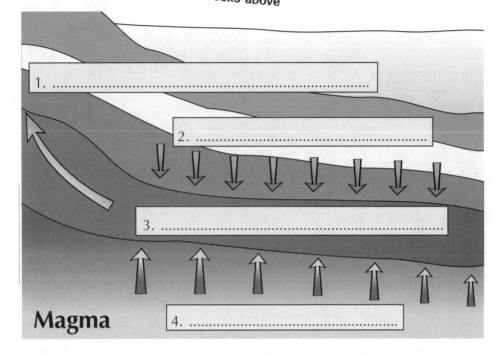

1. ....

2. ....

3. ....

Magma 4. ....

b) Describe the texture of metamorphic rock.

....

Q5 True or false? Tick the correct box.

		True	False
a)	Metamorphic rocks can be formed from igneous rocks.	☐	☐
b)	Sedimentary rocks only take a thousand years to form.	☐	☐
c)	Chalk is an igneous rock.	☐	☐
d)	Igneous rocks are softer than sedimentary rocks.	☐	☐
e)	Erosion can cause the shape of our landscape to change.	☐	☐

Q6 Explain why **fossils** are found in limestone and chalk.

....

....

....

Using Limestone

Q1 Calcium carbonate is quarried on a large scale because it's a raw material for several **building materials**.

Name three building materials made using limestone.

1. ....

2. ....

3. ....

Q2 Limestone is a useful rock but **quarrying** it causes some **problems**.

a) Describe two problems that quarrying limestone can cause.

1. ....

2. ....

b) Explain how limestone quarries may benefit the local community.

....

....

....

Q3 In Norway **powdered limestone** is added to lakes that have been damaged by acid rain.

a) Name the process that takes place when the powdered limestone reacts with the acid in the lake.

....

b) Explain why powdered limestone is also used in the chimneys at power stations.

....

....

....

Using Limestone

Q4 This passage is about **limestone extraction** in the Peak District National Park. Read the extract and then answer the questions that follow on the next page.

The Peak District National Park covers about 1500 km² of land. Tourism is very important — a lot of people visit the area to enjoy the countryside. Limestone quarrying is also part of the local economy and there are 12 large quarries in the park. Some people aren't keen

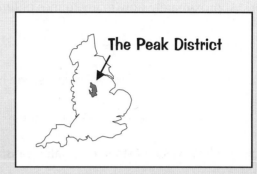

The Peak District

on all this — they say that quarrying is spoiling the natural beauty of the landscape, and discouraging tourists from visiting.

The limestone in the Peak District is very pure. It has been used locally in agriculture, and burned in lime kilns, for many years. When canals and railways were built in the area, limestone quarried in the park could be taken further afield, for use in industries elsewhere. This continues today, and is another cause for concern — large lorries clog up narrow roads and disturb the peace and quiet in small villages.

A lot of limestone has been dug out of the Peak District. In 2008, 7.9 million tonnes of limestone were quarried from the Peak District National Park — roughly five times as much as in 1951. This limestone is used in several different industries (the figures below are for 2008).

Use	Percentage
Aggregate (for road-building etc.)	52%
Cement	24%
Iron and steel making	2%
Chemicals and other uses	22%

Turn over the page for the questions about this article.

Using Limestone

a) What makes the **limestone** from the Peak District particularly useful?

....

b) Approximately how many tonnes of limestone were quarried in 1951?

....

c) Describe one way in which limestone has been used locally in the Peak District.

....

d) **i)** How was limestone originally **transported away** from the Peak District?

....

    ii) How is limestone **transported** today?

....

e) Do you think that the person who wrote the article is in favour of quarrying or against it? Explain the reasons for your answer.

....

....

f) Complete this table showing the amount of limestone quarried from the Peak District in 2008.

Use	Percentage	Total amount quarried in tonnes
Aggregate (for road-building etc.)	52%	
Cement	24%	
Iron and steel making	2%	
Chemicals and other uses	22%	

Limestone and Thermal Decomposition

Q1 Heating metal carbonates is an example of **thermal decomposition**.

a) Explain what **thermal decomposition** means.

....

b) **Calcium oxide** and **calcium carbonate** are both white solids.
How could you tell the difference between them?

....

c) How could you prove that carbon dioxide is produced when a metal carbonate is heated?

....

Q2 **Carbonates** decompose to form two products.

a) What is the chemical name for limestone?

....

b) Name the **two** products formed when limestone is heated.

1. ....

2. ....

c) What **solid** would be formed when **zinc carbonate** is heated?

....

d) Write a **word equation** for the reaction that occurs when **copper carbonate** is heated.

....

Q3 The hills of Northern England are dotted with the remains of **lime kilns** where **calcium carbonate** ($CaCO_3$) was heated by farmers to make **calcium oxide** (CaO).

a) Write a word equation for the reaction that takes place in a lime kiln.

....

b) Calcium oxide reacts violently with water to make calcium hydroxide ($Ca(OH)_2$).
Calcium hydroxide is a weak alkali.

What do farmers use calcium hydroxide for?

....

Limestone and Thermal Decomposition

Q4 Some carbonates thermally decompose more quickly than others.

a) You can carry out an experiment to find how easily some carbonates thermally decompose. Number the boxes 1 to 5 to put the method in order.

☐ Repeat for each carbonate.

☐ Compare your results.

☐ Pipe off the gas into a test tube of limewater.

☐ Heat the carbonate in a boiling tube.

☐ Record the time taken for the limewater to change colour.

b) Draw the **apparatus** used for this experiment in the box below.

c) i) How would you know which carbonate had decomposed the **fastest**?

....

ii) Why do carbonates decompose at **different** speeds?

....

d) Apart from the change in the limewater, what else might you notice when a carbonate thermally decomposes?

....

Atoms and Mass in Chemical Reactions

Q1 Use the words below to fill the gaps in the passage.
You might need to use some words more than once.

constant	atoms	rearranged	mass	particles

Elements and compounds are made up of .... and these are the

smallest .... you can get of each element.

It's the .... that take part in chemical reactions. During reactions they

aren't lost or made, they are just .... Because of this the

.... at the start and end of a reaction remains ....

Q2 When copper sulfate and sodium hydroxide react a **precipitate** forms.

a) What is a precipitate?

....

b) The precipitate formed is copper hydroxide. Write a **word equation** for this reaction.

....

c) If you started with 12 g of copper sulfate and 15 g of sodium hydroxide,
what would the total mass of the products be?

....

....

Q3 18 g of calcium oxide were reacted with some water.

a) The mass of the product at the end of the reaction was 29 g.
What mass of water was used?

....

....

b) Would you expect the properties of the product to be different from
the properties of the reactants?

....

Balancing Equations

Q1 Tick the boxes to show which of the following equations are **balanced** correctly.

		Correctly balanced	Incorrectly balanced
a)	$H_2 + Cl_2 \rightarrow 2HCl$	☐	☐
b)	$CuO + HCl \rightarrow CuCl_2 + H_2O$	☐	☐
c)	$N_2 + H_2 \rightarrow NH_3$	☐	☐
d)	$CuO + H_2 \rightarrow Cu + H_2O$	☐	☐
e)	$CaCO_3 \rightarrow CaO + CO_2$	☐	☐

Q2 Here is the equation for the formation of carbon **mon**oxide in a poorly ventilated gas fire. It is **not** balanced correctly.

$$C + O_2 \rightarrow CO$$

Circle the **correctly balanced** version of this equation.

$$C + O_2 \rightarrow CO_2$$

$$C + O_2 \rightarrow 2CO$$

$$2C + O_2 \rightarrow 2CO$$

Q3 In a book, this is the description of a reaction: "**methane** (CH_4) can be burnt in **oxygen** (O_2) to make **carbon dioxide** (CO_2) and **water** (H_2O)".

a) What are the **reactants** and the **products** in this reaction?

Reactants: ....   Products: ....

b) Write the **word equation** for this reaction.

....

c) Write the **balanced symbol equation** for the reaction.

....

Don't forget the oxygen ends up in both products

Top Tips: The most important thing to remember with balancing equations is that you can't change the **little numbers** — if you do that then you'll change the substance into something completely different. Just take your time and work through everything logically.

Balancing Equations

Q4 Write out the balanced **symbol** equations for the unbalanced picture equations below.

a) Na Na + Cl Cl → Na Cl / Na Cl

....

You can draw more pictures to help you balance the unbalanced ones.

b) Li + O O → Li O Li

....

c) Mg O C O O + H Cl → Cl Mg Cl + H O H + O C O

....

d) Li + H O H / H O H → Li O H + H H

....

Q5 Add **one** number to each of these equations so that they are **correctly balanced**.

a) $CuO + HBr \rightarrow CuBr_2 + H_2O$

b) $H_2 + Br_2 \rightarrow HBr$

c) $Mg + O_2 \rightarrow 2MgO$

d) $2NaOH + H_2SO_4 \rightarrow Na_2SO_4 + H_2O$

You need to have 2 bromines and 2 hydrogens on the left-hand side.

Q6 **Balance** these equations by adding in numbers.

a) $NaOH + AlBr_3 \rightarrow NaBr + Al(OH)_3$

b) $FeCl_2 + Cl_2 \rightarrow FeCl_3$

c) $N_2 + H_2 \rightarrow NH_3$

d) $Fe + O_2 \rightarrow Fe_2O_3$

e) $NH_3 + O_2 \rightarrow NO + H_2O$

$Fe_2O_3 + 3CO \rightarrow 2Fe + 3CO_2$

Mixed Questions — C1a Topics 1 & 2

Q1 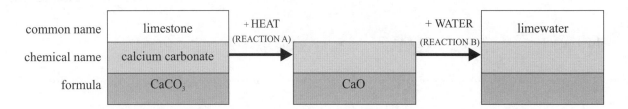 **Calcium carbonate** ($CaCO_3$), in the form of the rock **limestone**, is one of the most important raw materials for the chemical and construction industries.

a) Limestone can be processed to form **limewater**.

i) Complete the flow diagram.

		+HEAT (REACTION A)		+WATER (REACTION B)	
common name	limestone	→		→	limewater
chemical name	calcium carbonate				
formula	$CaCO_3$		CaO		

ii) Write a balanced symbol equation for reaction A.

.... → .... + ...

iii) Give one use of limewater.

....

b) Limestone can be processed to form useful building materials. Complete the flow diagram.

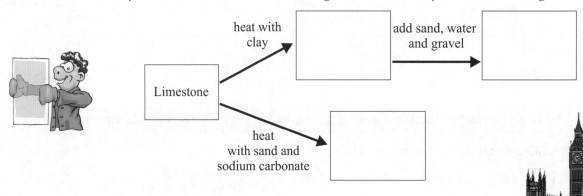

c) The limestone of the Houses of Parliament is crumbling away. What is causing the damage to the limestone and how?

....

d) Limestone is turned into **marble** by a natural process.

i) Describe this process.

....

....

ii) Give two ways in which marble is different from limestone.

1. ....

2. ....

Mixed Questions — C1a Topics 1 & 2

Q2 The graphs below give information about the Earth's atmosphere millions of years ago and today.

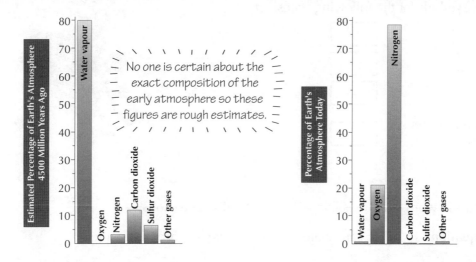

No one is certain about the exact composition of the early atmosphere so these figures are rough estimates.

a) Could the early atmosphere **support life** as we know it? Explain your answer.

....

....

b) Which **organisms** caused an increase in oxygen and a decrease in carbon dioxide?

....

c) Even though the level of **carbon dioxide** is much lower now than millions of years ago, in the last 250 years the level has **increased**. Complete the following passage by circling the correct words.

Humans are **increasing** / **decreasing** the amount of **carbon dioxide** / **oxygen** in the atmosphere by **burning** / **creating** fossil fuels. Also, deforestation **reduces** / **increases** the amount of carbon dioxide **absorbed** / **released** from the atmosphere.

d) Tick the correct boxes to indicate whether each statement is **true** or **false**.

True False

i) About 10% of the present atmosphere is noble gases, such as argon. ☐ ☐

ii) Very early in Earth's history volcanoes gave out gases. ☐ ☐

iii) Green plants take in oxygen and give out carbon dioxide during photosynthesis. ☐ ☐

e) Why is it difficult to be precise about the evolution of the atmosphere?

....

....

Mixed Questions — C1a Topics 1 & 2

Q3 State symbols give the **physical state** of a substance.

Give the **symbols** for the following states.

a) Solid ☐

b) Liquid ☐

c) Gas ☐

d) Dissolved in water (aqueous) ☐

Q4 Change these **word equations** into balanced **symbol equations**.

a) **Word equation:** zinc carbonate → zinc oxide + carbon dioxide

Symbol equation: ....

b) **Word equation:** copper + oxygen → copper oxide

Symbol equation: ....

c) **Word equation:** calcium oxide + water → calcium hydroxide

Symbol equation: ....

Q5 Bob thinks that the total mass in a reaction remains **constant**.

a) Describe an experiment using a precipitation reaction that he could do to prove this.

....

....

....

b) If he tried to prove that the total mass in a reaction remains constant using a thermal decomposition reaction of a carbonate, why would it be important to use sealed apparatus?

....

....

c) Explain why the mass of reactants always equals the mass of the products.

....

Hazard Symbols

Q1 True or false? Put a tick in the correct box.

		True	False
a)	Hazard symbols are found on the packaging of all chemicals.	☐	☐
b)	Hazard symbols show you what the dangers associated with a chemical are.	☐	☐
c)	All chemicals are toxic.	☐	☐
d)	Hazard symbols help you to choose safe-working procedures in the lab.	☐	☐
e)	You shouldn't use chemicals with more than three hazard symbols on the packaging.	☐	☐
f)	Hazard symbols are only found on chemicals that are extremely dangerous.	☐	☐
g)	You should always look at the hazard symbols for a chemical before using it.	☐	☐

Q2 Draw lines to match the **symbols** below with their **meanings** and **hazards**.

a) toxic — can cause death if swallowed, inhaled or absorbed through the skin

b) corrosive — causes reddening or blistering of the skin

c) highly flammable — provides oxygen which allows other materials to burn more fiercely

d) irritant — attacks and destroys living tissue

e) harmful — like toxic, but not quite as dangerous

f) oxidising — catches fire easily

Acids and Alkalis

Q1 Complete the following sentences about **acids** and **alkalis**.

a) Solutions which are not alkaline or neutral are said to be ....

b) A substance with a pH less than 7 is called an ....

c) A substance with a pH more than 7 is called a ....

d) An alkali is a base that dissolves in ....

e) The pH of pure water is ....

Q2 Draw lines to match **universal indicator colour** to **pH** value and **acid/alkali strength**.

UNIVERSAL INDICATOR COLOUR | pH | ACID/ALKALI STRENGTH

a) purple — 5/6 — strong alkali

b) yellow — 8/9 — weak alkali

c) dark green/blue — 14 — weak acid

d) red — 7 — neutral

e) green — 1 — strong acid

Q3 Ants' stings hurt because of the **formic acid** they release. The pH measurements of some household substances are given in the table.

Substance	pH
lemon juice	4
baking soda	9
caustic soda	14
soap powder	11

a) Suggest a substance from the list that could be used to relieve the discomfort of an ant sting.

....

Explain your answer.

....

....

b) Suggest why universal indicator only gives an **estimate** of pH.

....

....

Hydrochloric Acid and Indigestion Tablets

Q1 Fill in the blanks using the words below.

| base | indigestion | acidic | digestion | too much |
| neutralise | too little | alkaline | kill |

The stomach produces hydrochloric acid to help with .... The enzymes

which break down food in the stomach work best in an .... environment.

Having acid in the stomach also helps to .... bacteria — making it less

likely that you'll go down with some kind of nasty food poisoning. Indigestion is caused by

.... hydrochloric acid in the stomach. Indigestion tablets contain a

.... such as calcium carbonate, which will .... the acid.

Q2 **Antacid tablets** contain **alkalis** to neutralise the excess stomach acid that causes indigestion.

Joey wanted to test how well different antacid tablets neutralise acid. He dissolved each type of tablet in distilled water and added a few drops of indicator. Joey put hydrochloric acid in a burette and added it to the antacid tablet solution until it had been neutralised. He then read off how much acid was left in the burette. His results for five different tablets are shown in the table below.

Tablet	Volume of HCl at start of experiment / cm³	Volume of HCl left at end of experiment / cm³	Volume of HCl needed to neutralise tablet / cm³
A	50.0	35.2	14.8
B	46.9	31.0	
C	37.5	14.1	
D	49.3	32.6	
E	42.2	35.6	

a) Complete the table to show the amount of acid required to neutralise each tablet. The first one has been done for you.

b) Which tablet requires the smallest amount of acid to neutralise it?

....

c) One of the antacids requires you to take **two** tablets as a **single dose**. The others require you to take just one. Which of the antacids, A to E, do you think requires two tablets?

....

d) Which tablet is most effective in a **single dose**? Explain your answer.

....

....

Reactions of Acids

Q1 Give the **general word equation** for the reaction between an **acid** and a **metal hydroxide**.

....

Q2 Give the **general word equation** for the reaction between an **acid** and a **metal oxide**.

....

Q3 Fill in the blanks to complete the word equations for **acids** reacting with **metal oxides** and **metal hydroxides**.

a) hydrochloric acid + lead oxide → .... chloride + water

b) nitric acid + copper hydroxide → copper .... + water

c) sulfuric acid + zinc oxide → zinc sulfate + ...

d) hydrochloric acid + ... oxide → nickel .... + ...

e) .... acid + copper oxide → .... nitrate + ...

f) sulfuric acid + ... hydroxide →

sodium .... + ...

g) hydrochloric acid + ... hydroxide →

calcium .... + ...

Reactions of Acids

Q4 **Complete** the following equations.

a) $H_2SO_{4(aq)}$ + ... $\rightarrow$ $CuSO_{4(aq)}$ + $H_2O_{(l)}$

b) $2HNO_{3(aq)}$ + $MgO_{(s)}$ $\rightarrow$ $Mg(NO_3)_{2(aq)}$ + ...

c) .... + $KOH_{(aq)}$ $\rightarrow$ $KCl_{(aq)}$ + $H_2O_{(l)}$

d) $2HCl_{(aq)}$ + ... $\rightarrow$ $ZnCl_{2(aq)}$ + $H_2O_{(l)}$

e) $H_2SO_{4(aq)}$ + $2NaOH_{(aq)}$ $\rightarrow$ .... + ...

f) $HNO_{3(aq)}$ + $KOH_{(s)}$ $\rightarrow$ .... + ...

g) .... + $ZnO_{(s)}$ $\rightarrow$ $ZnSO_{4(aq)}$ + ...

Q5 **Balance** the following acid/base reactions.

a) H_3PO_4 + $NaOH$ $\rightarrow$ Na_3PO_4 + H_2O

b) $NaOH$ + H_2SO_4 $\rightarrow$ Na_2SO_4 + H_2O

c) $Mg(OH)_2$ + HNO_3 $\rightarrow$ $Mg(NO_3)_2$ + H_2O

d) NH_3 + H_2SO_4 $\rightarrow$ $(NH_4)_2SO_4$

Reactions of Acids

Q6   Give the **general word equation** for the reaction between an **acid** and a **metal carbonate**.

....

Q7   Complete the following word equations for **acids** reacting with **metal carbonates**.

a)   Nitric acid + sodium carbonate →

.... + ... + ...

b)   Calcium carbonate + hydrochloric acid →

.... + ... + ...

c)   .... + sulfuric acid →

zinc sulfate + ... + ...

d)   Nitric acid + ... →

magnesium nitrate + ... + ...

e)   Copper carbonate + ... →

copper chloride + ... + ...

f)   .... + ... →

magnesium sulfate + ... + ...

Top Tips: Take your time over these — it's easy to zip through them and misread the names of the compounds. Think logically — you can't have any elements in the products that weren't there at the start of the reaction. If you get stuck check back over the general word equation.

Reactions of Acids

Q8 Fill in the blanks in the following statements about **metal** and **acid** reactions.

a) Hydrochloric acid always gives .... salts.

b) Nitric acid always gives .... salts.

c) Sulfuric acid always gives .... salts.

Q9 **Complete** the following symbol equations. Remember to include state symbols.

a) $H_2SO_{4(aq)} + ... \rightarrow CuSO_{4(aq)} + H_2O_{(l)} + CO_{2(g)}$

b) $2HNO_{3(aq)} + ... \rightarrow Mg(NO_3)_{2(aq)} + H_2O + ...$

c) $2HCl_{(aq)} + ... \rightarrow ZnCl_{2(aq)} + H_2O_{(l)} + CO_{2(g)}$

d) $H_2SO_{4(aq)} + Na_2CO_{3(aq)} \rightarrow .... + ... + ...$

Q10 **Balance** the following acid/base reactions.

a) $HCl + CaCO_3 \rightarrow CaCl_2 + H_2O + CO_2$

b) $HCl + K_2CO_3 \rightarrow KCl + H_2O + CO_2$

c) $HNO_3 + ZnCO_3 \rightarrow Zn(NO_3)_2 + H_2O + CO_2$

d) $Na_2CO_3 + HCl \rightarrow NaCl + H_2O + CO_2$

Electrolysis

Q1 Fill in the blanks in the passage below using the words provided.

	direct current		gas	
electrical energy		electrodes		electrolyte

Electrolysis is the breaking down (decomposition) of a compound using

.... The electricity used comes from a ....

source, such as a battery. It requires a liquid to conduct the electricity, called

an .... The electricity is applied to the liquid by two

.... The electrolyte contains the compound, which is broken

down into its component parts. The component parts are released as atoms or molecules

— often as a ....

Q2 Electrolysis of dilute **hydrochloric acid** gives **two** gases.

a) Name the two gases produced.

Gas 1: ....   Gas 2: ....

b) Describe a simple **laboratory test** you would use to identify each of the gases.

Test for gas 1 ....

....

Test for gas 2 ....

....

Q3 After electrolysing a salt solution, Englebert noticed that the laboratory had a similar smell to his local **swimming pool**.

Think about the uses of chlorine.

a) Suggest why this was. ....

....

b) Explain why this could be a safety issue.

....

c) Suggest what could be done in future to make this experiment safer.

....

Electrolysis

Q4   Harry runs a little **sea water electrolysis** business from his garden shed.
He keeps a record of all the different **industries** that he sells his products to.

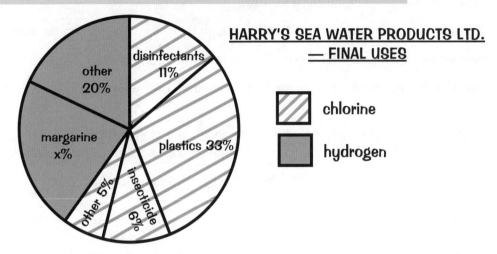

a)   Which sea water product does Harry sell the most of?

....

b)   What percentage of Harry's products are used to manufacture **margarine**?

....

c)   Which **industry** uses the biggest proportion of Harry's products?

....

Q5   Sammy decides to carry out the electrolysis of **water** in his bedroom.

a)   Name the two gases produced by the electrolysis of water.

....

b)   Sammy's mother is worried that he's doing a dangerous experiment using concentrated
hydrochloric acid. Sammy says that he can prove her wrong by testing the gases given off.
Explain what he would do and what it would show.

....

....

....

....

....

....

Metal Ores

Q1 Indicate whether each of the statements below about **metal ores** is true or false.

True False

a) Metal ores are found in the Earth's crust. ☐ ☐

b) Ores are metal compounds that contain enough metal to make extraction worthwhile. ☐ ☐

c) The more reactive the metal, the easier it is to extract from its ore. ☐ ☐

d) Zinc and iron can both be extracted by heating their ores with carbon. ☐ ☐

Q2 Copper may have been formed when someone accidentally dropped some copper ore into a **wood fire**. When the ashes were cleared away some copper was left.

Explain how dropping the ore into the fire led to the extraction of copper.

....

....

Remember that wood contains carbon.

Q3 Fill in the blanks in the passage below.

.... can be used to extract metals that are

.... it in the reactivity series. Oxygen is removed

from the metal oxide in a process called ....

Other metals have to be extracted using .... because

they are .... reactive.

Q4 Some metals are found as **ores**. Others, such as gold, are usually found as **elements**.

a) Explain why gold is usually found as an element.

....

b) i) One type of iron ore is magnetite (Fe_3O_4).
Write a balanced symbol equation for its formation from iron (Fe) and oxygen (O_2).

....

ii) Is the iron **oxidised** or **reduced** in this reaction? ....

c) i) Write a balanced symbol equation to show the reaction that happens when copper is extracted from its ore, CuO, using carbon.

....

ii) Is the copper **oxidised** or **reduced** in this reaction? ....

Reduction of Metal Ores

Q1 Some metals can be **extracted** by heating their ore with **carbon**.

a) Explain why **iron** can be extracted from iron oxide by heating with **carbon**.

....

b) Write the **word equation** for the reduction of iron oxide with carbon.

....

c) **Complete** and **balance** the symbol equation for this reaction.

......Fe_2O_3 + ... → .... + ...

d) Not all metals can be extracted using this method.
Tick the boxes below to show which metals **cannot** be extracted this way.

Potassium ☐

Magnesium ☐

Tin ☐

Calcium ☐

Aluminium ☐

Sodium ☐

Lead ☐

Q2 Read the following passage about **zinc** extraction then answer the questions below.

Zinc is most commonly found as the ore sphalerite (mainly zinc sulfide, ZnS).

The sphalerite is first processed to remove impurities such as iron, copper and lead sulfides.

Then it is converted to zinc oxide and sulfur dioxide by heating it with air.

Finally, the zinc oxide is reduced by heating it to 950 °C with carbon.

a) What is the **name** and **chemical formula** of the most common zinc ore?

Name .... Chemical formula ....

b) Write a **word equation** for the conversion of this ore to zinc oxide.

....

c) Give the balanced **symbol equation** for the reaction of **zinc oxide** with carbon.

....

Reduction of Metal Ores

Q3 Draw lines to join these words with their correct meanings.

Electrolysis — Used to apply electricity to the liquid.

Electrolyte — The breakdown of a substance using electricity.

Electrode — The liquid that is used in electrolysis.

Q4 Are these statements about the extraction of **aluminium** true or false?

True False

a) Substances can only be electrolysed if they're molten or in solution. ☐ ☐

b) Aluminium is extracted from its ore, bauxite. ☐ ☐

c) Hydrogen gas is given off during the extraction of aluminium by electrolysis. ☐ ☐

d) Aluminium is collected at the electrodes. ☐ ☐

e) Aluminium has to be extracted by electrolysis because it's lower than carbon in the reactivity series. ☐ ☐

Q5 The diagram below shows the electrolysis of **aluminium oxide**.

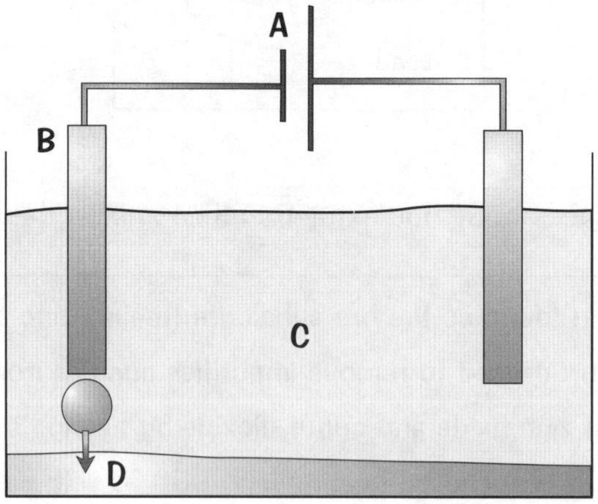

Write the labels that should go at points A–D using **some** of the words below.

electrode   aluminium solution   mains electricity   molten aluminium

molten aluminium oxide   d.c. source   aluminium oxide solution

A ....

B ....

C ....

D ....

Properties of Metals

Q1   This table shows some of the **properties** of four different **metals**.

Metal	Heat conduction	Cost	Resistance to corrosion	Strength
1	average	high	excellent	good
2	average	medium	good	excellent
3	excellent	low	good	good
4	low	high	average	poor

Use the information in the table to choose which metal would be **best** for making each of the following:

a)   Saucepan bases ....

b)   Car bodies ....

Think about how long a statue would have to last for.

c)   A statue to be placed in a town centre ....

Q2   What **properties** would you look for if you were asked to choose a **metal** suitable for making knives and forks?

    ....

    ....

    ....

Q3   For each of the following **applications** of metals, say which **property** of the metal makes it ideal for the given use. Choose the best answer from the list of typical properties of metals below. You may only use each property **once**.

        ductile   low density   resists corrosion   conducts heat

a)   Aluminium is used to make aircraft.   ....

b)   Copper is used to make the base of saucepans and frying pans.   ....

c)   Gold is used by dentists to make long-lasting fillings and false teeth. ....

d)   Copper is drawn out into thin wires for electrical cables.   ....

Top Tips: Remember most elements are metals and most metals have similar properties. But don't be a fool and think they're all identical — there are lots of little differences which make them useful for different things. Some metals are pretty weird, for example mercury is liquid at room temperature, which means it's not ideal for making cars.

Properties of Metals

Q4 In an experiment some identically sized rods of different materials (A, B, C and D) were **heated** at one end and **temperature sensors** were connected to the other ends. The results are shown in the graph.

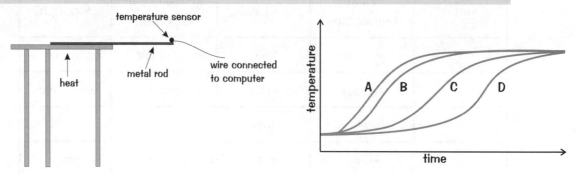

a) Which two rods do you think were made from metals?

....

b) Which of the metals was the best conductor of heat and how can you tell?

....

Q5 Imagine that a space probe has brought a sample of a new element back from Mars. Scientists think that the element is a **metal**, but they aren't certain. Give **three properties** they could look for to provide evidence that the element is a **metal**.

1. ....

2. ....

3. ....

Q6 Use some of the words below to **complete** this passage about corrosion. You can only use each word once.

all	less	dissolved	slowly	oxidised
more	easily	some	reduced	

Over time, ... metals corrode. Corrosion happens because

the metal is being .... Metals which are high in the reactivity

series are .... likely to corrode because they react more

.... with oxygen. For example, iron is ....

corrosion-resistant than lead.

Making Metals More Useful

Q1 Most iron is made into the alloy **steel**.

a) Write a definition of the term '**alloy**'.

....

....

b) How is **iron** turned into **steel**?

....

....

Tonight Matthew, I'm going to be... steel.

Q2 Draw lines to connect the correct phrases in each column. One has been done for you.

Metal / Alloy	What has been added	Use
low-carbon steel	nothing	blades for tools
iron from a blast furnace	chromium	cutlery
high-carbon steel	0.1% carbon	car bodies
stainless steel	1.5% carbon	ornamental railings

Q3 Complete the following sentences using some of the metals below.

gold copper platinum titanium nickel iron zinc

a) Nitinol is an alloy that contains .... and ....

b) To make gold hard enough for jewellery it is mixed with metals such as

.... , ... and ....

c) Gold alloys are measured in carats, which indicates the proportion of pure ....

Making Metals More Useful

Q4 24-carat gold is **pure** gold. 9-carat gold contains **9 parts** gold to 15 parts other metals. 9-carat gold is **harder** and **cheaper** than 24-carat gold.

a) What percentage of 9-carat gold is actually gold?

....

b) Why is 9-carat gold harder than pure gold?

....

....

Q5 Gold alloys can be described by **carats** or **fineness**.

a) Explain what 'fineness' means.

....

b) Use lines to link the correct parts of the following sentences.

900 fineness is the same as   1 carat gold.

042 fineness is the same as   a gold alloy with 25% other metals.

375 fineness is the same as   9 carat gold.

750 fineness is the same as   90% pure gold.

Q6 Recently, scientists have been developing **smart alloys**.

a) Give an example of a use for smart alloys.

....

Smart Alloy of the Month Award

Presented to: _Nitinol_

Presented by: _CGP_

b) i) Name **one** property which some smart alloys have that normal alloys don't.

....

ii) What **advantage** does this give smart alloys?

....

....

Top Tips: As you must know by now, metals have lots of pretty useful properties, but they can be made even more useful by being mixed together to make alloys. However, it's possible to go one step further and make smart alloys. The clue's in the name — they're like normal alloys, but smarter.

Recycling

Q1 Give **three** advantages of **recycling metals**.

1. ....

2. ....

3. ....

Q2 Tick the correct boxes to show whether the following statements are **true** or **false**.

	True	False

a) Recycling could help to prevent further increases in greenhouse gas levels. ☐ ☐

b) It is important to recycle copper because there is a finite amount available. ☐ ☐

c) Recycling costs nothing and has huge benefits for the environment. ☐ ☐

Q3 Below is some information about **aluminium**, a widely used metal today.

> Bauxite (aluminium ore) gives 1 kg of aluminium for every 4 kg of bauxite mined.
> Bauxite mines are often located in rainforests.
> Extracting aluminium from bauxite requires huge quantities of electricity.
> An aluminium can weighs about 20 g.

a) i) How much ore has to be mined to produce 1 tonne (1000 kg) of aluminium?

....

ii) Australians used about 3 billion aluminium cans in 2002.
How many tonnes of aluminium does this represent?

....

iii) How many tonnes of bauxite were mined to supply Australians with aluminium cans in 2002?

....

b) Outline the **environmental** consequences of:

i) Mining the bauxite. ....

....

ii) Extracting the aluminium. ....

....

iii) Not recycling the cans. ....

....

C1b Topic 5 — Fuels

Fractional Distillation of Crude Oil

Q1   Circle the correct words to complete these sentences.

a)   Crude oil is a **mixture** / **compound** of different molecules.

b)   Crude oil contains **carbohydrate** / **hydrocarbon** molecules.

c)   The molecules in crude oil **are** / **aren't** chemically bonded to each other.

d)   Physical methods **can** / **can't** be used to separate out the molecules in crude oil.

Q2   Name the two elements that **hydrocarbons** are made up of.

....

Q3   The molecules listed below are in order of **smallest** to **largest** from left to right.
Label this diagram of a **fractionating column** to show where these substances can be collected.

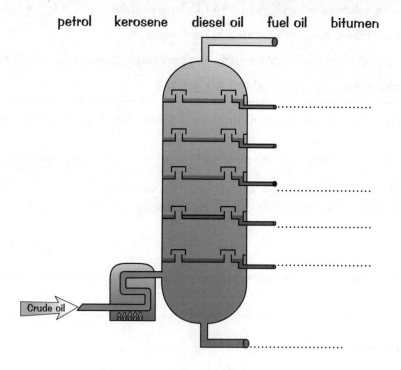

petrol   kerosene   diesel oil   fuel oil   bitumen

Q4   What is the connection between the **size** of the **molecules** in crude oil and their **condensing** (or **boiling**) points?

....

....

Fractional Distillation of Crude Oil

Q5   Draw lines to match up each crude oil **fraction** to its most common use.

Fraction	Use
Gas	Used to surface roads and roofs
Petrol	Used as a fuel for lorries, trains and some cars
Kerosene	Used as an aircraft fuel
Diesel Oil	Used for cooking and heating
Fuel Oil	Used as a fuel for cars
Bitumen	Used as a fuel for ships and some power stations

phwoar... nice tank, love

Q6   Use some of the words below to fill the gaps in the passage.

viscous   chlorine   carbon   lower   ignite   hydrogen   higher

Fractions that are tapped off at the top of the fractionating column have .... boiling points than fractions tapped off at the bottom.

They also have fewer .... and .... atoms.

The shorter the molecules in the fraction, the more easily they ....

Also the shorter the molecules the less .... they are.

Q7   Petrol is a **non-renewable** fossil fuel.

Explain why petrol is **non-renewable**.

....

....

....

Top Tips: So many of the things around us that we take for granted are made from the products of crude oil. It's a bit of a pain really 'cos that's why the examiner thinks it's important. Remember that the length of a hydrocarbon molecule affects its boiling point and how flammable it is. Oh, and for extra marks, don't forget to learn the uses of all those lovely fractions too.

Burning Fuels

Q1   Answer the following questions about **burning hydrocarbons**.

a)   Write a **word equation** for the complete combustion of a hydrocarbon.

....

b)   Circle the correct words from each pair in the sentences below.

> When a hydrocarbon is burnt, the carbon and hydrogen are **oxidised / reduced.**
>
> The reaction **gives out / takes in** energy

Q2   When choosing fuels there are a number of **factors** which must be taken into consideration. Give three factors that are important when choosing a fuel to be used in a car engine.

1. ....

2. ....

3. ....

Q3   Answer the following questions about **hydrocarbons**.

a)   Underline the two correct formulae for the products of the complete combustion of a hydrocarbon.

H_2S CH_4 CO_2 SO_2 H_2O

b)   Suggest why a fuel might not burn completely.

....

....

My favourite few L's

L L L L L

Q4   **Incomplete combustion** can cause problems.

a)   Fill in the blanks to complete the word equation for the incomplete combustion of hydrocarbons.

hydrocarbon + oxygen → .... + ...

+ .... + ...

b)   Why is it dangerous if incomplete combustion occurs in household gas appliances?

....

....

Environmental Problems

Q1   Explain why **sulfur dioxide** is produced when some hydrocarbons are burnt.

....

....

Q2   Draw lines to link the correct parts of these sentences.

| The main cause of acid rain is | acid rain. |

| Acid rain kills trees and | sulfuric acid. |

| Limestone buildings and statues are affected by | acidifies lakes. |

| In clouds sulfur dioxide reacts with water to make | sulfur dioxide. |

Q3   Give **three** ways that the amount of **acid rain** can be reduced.

1. ....

2. ....

3. ....

Q4   Scientists are working hard to develop **new technologies** that are environmentally friendly.

Do you think it is solely the responsibility of scientists to find ways of reducing environmental damage or should people be prepared to change their lifestyles too? Explain your answer.

....

....

There's no right or wrong answer here — the key is being able to explain your reasoning.

....

Top Tips: Don't panic, acid rain won't burn your skin off. That said, it's not your average harmless old drizzle either — it has far reaching effects, as the pollutants that cause it can get carried a long way. Plus, there are soot particles, carbon monoxide and carbon dioxide to think about as well. All in all, burning hydrocarbons is a dirty business and we'll need to clean up our act sooner or later.

90

More Environmental Problems

Q1 Underline the statements below about the greenhouse effect that are **true**.

- The greenhouse effect is needed for life on Earth as we know it.

- Greenhouse gases include carbon dioxide and methane.

- Human activity isn't affecting the amount of greenhouse gases.

- Increasing amounts of greenhouse gases are causing global warming.

Q2 The graph shows the average temperature of the Earth between **1961** and **1990**, and how the temperature has differed from it over the last **150 years**.

Variation from average global temperature (°C)

variation from average

average temp. (1961-1990)

0.6, 0.4, 0.2, 0, -0.2, -0.4, -0.6

1850 1900 1950 2000

a) Describe what trend the graph shows.

....

....

....

b) Name two human activities thought to be causing this change in temperature.

1. ....

2. ....

c) Suggest why the graph shows data from the last 150 years and not just the last ten years.

....

....

Q3 Circle the correct words from each pair to complete the passage below.

The consensus among climate scientists is that the use of **fossil / nuclear** fuels is linked to **a decrease / an increase** in the world's temperature. This is because when these fuels are burned, they give off **ozone / CO_2**, which is a **greenhouse / radioactive** gas.

C1b Topic 5 — Fuels

More Environmental Problems

Q4   **Carbon dioxide** and **methane** are two atmospheric gases which are important in the regulation of the Earth's **temperature**.

a)   Which of A, B, C and D best explains how CO_2 and methane help regulate the Earth's temperature? Circle your answer.

  A They absorb heat from the Sun.   **B** They keep the polar ice caps from melting.

  C They absorb heat from the Earth.   **D** They counteract acid rain.

b)   Explain how you add to carbon dioxide production if:

  i) you are driven to school in a car instead of walking.

  ....

  ii) you leave the TV on standby all night.

  ....

Q5   Tick the boxes to show whether the following statements are **true** or **false**.

		True	False
a)	Oxygen is released when trees are burnt to clear the land.	☐	☐
b)	Living trees remove CO_2 from the atmosphere during photosynthesis.	☐	☐
c)	Chopping down trees helps to reduce carbon dioxide levels.	☐	☐

Q6   Scientists are researching new ways to **remove** CO_2 from the atmosphere.

a)   Use the words below to fill the gaps in the passage.

high   photosynthesis   seeding   hydrocarbons   phytoplankton   injecting
Iron .... involves .... iron into the upper ocean to encourage blooms of .... These blooms remove CO_2 from the atmosphere during .... and so could help to restore the balance. Converting carbon dioxide into .... using .... temperature and pressure, and a catalyst, is another method being researched by scientists.

b)   Give **one** possible disadvantage of **one** of the methods described in the passage above.

....

....

92

Biofuels

Q1   What are **biofuels**?

....

....

Q2   **Biogas** is an example of a biofuel.
The diagram shows the production and use of one type of biogas.

a)   Label the diagram by writing the correct
letter in the boxes next to the arrows:

A CO_2 released into atmosphere

B biogas generator

C animal waste

D CO_2 absorbed by grass during photosynthesis

E methane $\rightarrow CO_2$

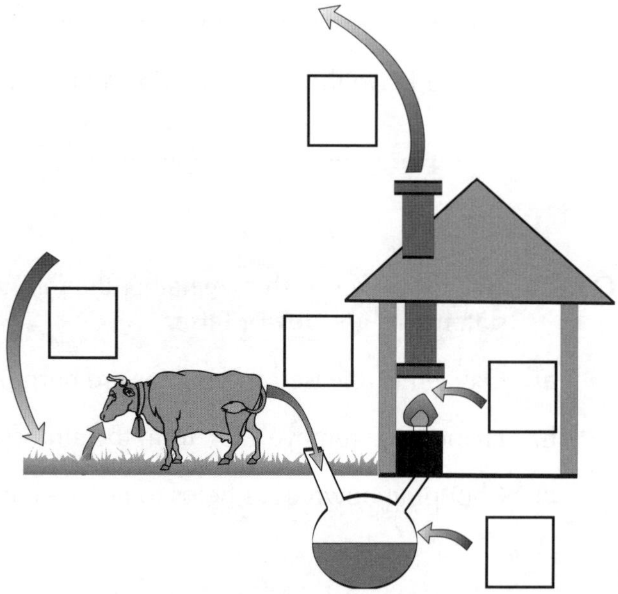

b)   Explain why biogas is a renewable fuel.

....

c)   Suggest why biogas is a fairly cheap fuel.

....

....

Q3   Indicate by ticking the box whether these statements are **true** or **false**.

		True	False
a)	Ethanol can be used as fuel.	☐	☐
b)	Ethanol is produced by fermenting sugar with yeast.	☐	☐
c)	Ethanol burns to give off toxic gases.	☐	☐
d)	Cars can be adapted to run on a mixture of 50% ethanol and 50% petrol.	☐	☐
e)	It doesn't take any energy to produce ethanol.	☐	☐

Biofuels

Q4   In Brazil, **ethanol** produced by **fermenting sugar cane** is a popular fuel for vehicles. The ethanol is mixed with **petrol** before it is used to give a fuel known as **gasohol**.

a)   What is produced when **ethanol** (C_2H_5OH) is burnt?

....

b)   Using gasohol does not increase the amount of carbon dioxide in the atmosphere as much as using pure petrol does. Explain why not.

....

....

c)   Why would it be more difficult to produce large quantities of gasohol in the UK than it is in Brazil?

....

....

Q5   Alternative fuels such as **biogas** and **gasohol** have advantages and disadvantages compared with traditional fossil fuels.

Imagine you are writing a leaflet for a 'green' organisation promoting the use of alternative fuels like biogas and ethanol instead of fossil fuels.

a)   Give four advantages of these fuels that you could use in favour of your argument.

1. ....

2. ....

3. ....

4. ....

b)   Suggest two points that someone who disagrees with you might put forward.

1. ....

....

2. ....

....

Top Tips: **Reducing CO_2 emissions** isn't all about loving trees and hugging bunnies, but about being sensible. No one wants to go back to living in caves, but we do need to face up to the fact that our modern lifestyle is causing problems. Luckily there might be some real solutions in the pipeline.

Fuel Cells

Q1   Hydrogen and oxygen can be used in fuel cells.

  a)   Draw lines to match the gases with the laboratory tests for them.

| Oxygen | | Relights a glowing splint |
| Hydrogen | | Makes a squeaky pop when burnt |

  b)   Name the product obtained when hydrogen and oxygen react in a fuel cell.

  ....

Q2   Use some of the words in the box to complete the passage below.

| fuel | battery | oxygen | electricity | carbon dioxide | walrus |

A fuel cell is an electrical cell that's supplied with a .... and

.... and uses energy from the reaction between them to

generate ....

Q3   Give three **advantages** and two **disadvantages** of using hydrogen fuel cells compared to alternative energy sources.

Advantages:

1. ....

2. ....

3. ....

Disadvantages:

1. ....

2. ....

Measuring the Energy Content of Fuels

Q1 Isobella is trying to decide which hydrocarbon, A or B, is the best one to use as a fuel. She tests the **energy content** of the hydrocarbons by using them to heat 50 cm³ of water from 25 °C to 40 °C. The results of this experiment are shown in the table.

Hydrocarbon	Initial Mass (g)	Final Mass (g)	Mass of Fuel Burnt (g)
A	98	92	
B	102	89	

a) Complete the table by calculating the mass of fuel that was burned in each case.

b) i) Which hydrocarbon would be the best to use as a fuel?

....

ii) Explain your answer.

....

c) i) The apparatus that Isobella used is shown below. Fill in the missing labels.

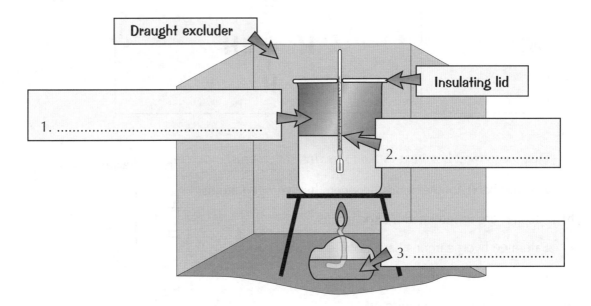

Draught excluder

Insulating lid

1. ....

2. ....

3. ....

ii) Explain the purpose of the draught excluder and the insulating lid in the diagram above.

....

d) Give three things that Isobella should keep **the same** to make sure that her experiment is **fair**.

1. ....

2. ....

3. ....

96

Alkanes and Alkenes

Q1 **Alkanes** and **alkenes** are both hydrocarbons.

Complete the table below to show the names and displayed formulae of some alkanes and alkenes.

Name	Displayed formula
a)	
ethane	**b)**
c)	

The displayed formula just shows how all the atoms are arranged.

Q2 Tick the correct box next to the following statements.

		True	False
a)	Alkenes have double bonds between the hydrogen atoms.	☐	☐
b)	Alkenes are unsaturated hydrocarbons.	☐	☐
c)	Saturated hydrocarbons have double bonds.	☐	☐
d)	Ethene has two carbon atoms.	☐	☐
e)	Alkanes are found in crude oil.	☐	☐

Q3 Fill in the gaps using the words below. You might need to use some words more than once.

brown	bromine water	green	colourless	decolourise	limewater

You can test for alkenes by adding them to ....

An alkene will .... the ...., turning it from

.... to ....

C1b Topic 5 — Fuels

Cracking Hydrocarbons

Q1   Fill in the gaps by choosing from the words in the box.

high	shorter	long	saturated	catalyst	cracking
diesel	molecules	petrol	double bond		alkenes

There is more need for .... chain fractions of crude oil such as

.... than for longer chains such as ....

Heating .... hydrocarbon molecules to .... temperatures

with a .... breaks them down into smaller ....

This is called .... It also produces .... which are

needed for making plastics.

Q2   This apparatus can be used to crack a **liquid hydrocarbon** such as **paraffin**.

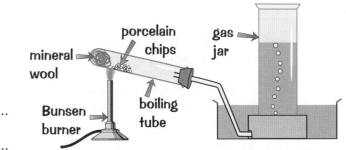

a)   Where would the paraffin be?

....

....

b)   What are the porcelain chips for?

....

c)   What collects in the gas jar?

....

Q3   Change this diagram into a **symbol equation**.

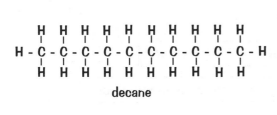

decane

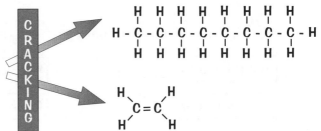

Symbol equation: .... → .... + ...

Using Alkenes to Make Polymers

Q1 The equation below shows a polymerisation reaction to form **poly(ethene)**.

$$n \begin{pmatrix} H & H \\ | & | \\ C = C \\ | & | \\ H & H \end{pmatrix} \longrightarrow \begin{pmatrix} H & H \\ | & | \\ \!-\!C - C\!-\! \\ | & | \\ H & H \end{pmatrix}_n$$

poly(ethene)

a) What is the name of the monomer used to form poly(ethene)?

....

b) Draw a similar equation below to show the polymerisation of propene (C_3H_6).

It's easier if you think of propene as

$$\underset{H}{\overset{H}{\diagdown}} C = C \underset{CH_3}{\overset{H}{\diagup}}$$

Q2 The diagram shows part of the chain of a **poly(chloroethene)** (**PVC**) molecule.

$$\begin{array}{cccccccccccc} & H & & Cl & & H & & Cl & & H & & Cl \\ & | & & | & & | & & | & & | & & | \\ -\!C\!-\!&C\!-\!&C\!-\!&C\!-\!&C\!-\!&C\!-\! \\ & | & & | & & | & & | & & | & & | \\ & H & & H & & H & & H & & H & & H \end{array}$$

a) Which of these formulae represents the monomer used to make PVC? Tick one box.

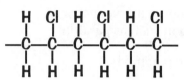

b) Write a displayed equation to show the formation of PVC.

A displayed equation just shows how all the atoms are arranged — like the one in Q1.

Q3 Draw lines to match up each **polymer** to its use.

Poly(ethene)		Non-stick coating for pans
Poly(propene)		Clothing, electric cables and pipes
Poly(chloroethene), PVC		Plastic bags
PTFE		Carpets, thermal underwear and plastic containers

Using Alkenes to Make Polymers

Q4   Fractional distillation of crude oil produces useful fractions and not-so-useful fractions.
The not-so-useful ones are **cracked** to form alkenes. Alkenes can be **polymerised** to make plastics.

Write down the differences between cracking and polymerisation.

We bring you gold, frankincense...
and poly-myrrh

....

....

....

....

Q5   Most polymers are **not** biodegradable.

If something's biodegradable it can rot.

a) What problems does this cause for the environment?

....

....

b) What is the problem with burning polymers to dispose of them?

....

c) Give **two** problems with recycling polymers.

1. ....

2. ....

d) Scientists are working on making biodegradable materials from genetically modified plants.
Suggest why tests need to be carried out to find out what happens when the polymer breaks down.

....

....

Top Tips: Sorry, but **polymers** are all over the blooming place, so you're going to have to be
clued up about them. It's really no biggie though, because if you think about it, they're just glorified
daisy chains. A bunch of silly hydrogen and carbon atoms standing around holding hands with each
other — maybe with some chlorine or something as well. What a load of fuss for a plastic cup.

Mixed Questions — C1b Topics 3, 4 & 5

Q1   Metals make up about 80% of all the elements in the periodic table.

a)   Read each of the following statements about metals. If the statement is true, tick the box.

☐ Metals are generally strong but also bendy.

☐ Metals corrode when they are oxidised.

☐ Generally, metals have low melting and boiling points.

☐ Properties of a metal can be altered by mixing it with another metal to form an alloy.

b) i)   Copper is used for water pipes. Give one reason why it is good for this.

....

....

ii) Give one use of gold and say why it is suitable for this use.

....

....

c)   Look at the information in the table below. R, S, T and U are all metals.

Material	Strength	Cost (£)	Density (g/cm³)	Melting Point (°C)
R	High	100	3	1000
S	Medium	90	5	150
T	High	450	8	1200
U	Low	200	11	1070

Explain in detail which material would be most suitable to build an aeroplane body.

....

....

....

Q2   **Biogas** is a renewable fuel.

a)   What is biogas made from? ....

b)   Explain why burning biogas produces **no net increase** in atmospheric carbon dioxide.

....

....

Mixed Questions — C1b Topics 3, 4 & 5

Q3   The metals **aluminium**, **copper** and **iron** can be extracted from their **ores**.

a)   Metal ores are often described as 'finite resources'. Explain the term 'finite resource'.

....

b)   The table shows the reactivity series of metals and dates of discovery.

i)   What pattern can be seen in the data?

....

....

ii) Suggest an explanation for this.

....

....

....

....

metal	discovery	
potassium	AD 1807	most reactive
sodium	AD 1807	
calcium	AD 1808	
magnesium	AD 1755	
aluminium	AD 1825	
carbon		
zinc	about AD 1400	
iron	about 2500 BC	
tin	about 2000 BC	
lead	about 3500 BC	
hydrogen		
copper	about 4200 BC	
silver	about 4000 BC	
gold	about 6000 BC	
platinum	before 1500 BC	least reactive

c)   i)   Complete the word equation for the reduction of iron ore with carbon.

iron oxide   + ...   →   **iron**   + ...

ii) Write a **balanced symbol equation** for this reaction. (The formula of iron oxide is Fe_2O_3.)

....

d)   Copper metal can be extracted from its ore and used in electrical wiring.
Give **two** physical properties of copper that make it suitable for this use.

1. ....

2. ....

e)   One of the most common elements present in the Earth's crust is aluminium

i)   What is the main ore of aluminium called?

....

ii) Explain why aluminium metal can only be extracted using electrolysis.

....

....

Mixed Questions — C1b Topics 3, 4 & 5

Q4   **Petrol** and **diesel** are two commonly used fuels for cars.

a) Diesel has longer molecules than petrol. List **two** differences you would expect in physical properties between petrol and diesel.

1. ....

2. ....

b) Ethanol is an alternative fuel to petrol and diesel.

i) How can ethanol be produced?

....

ii) Why is ethanol a more environmentally friendly fuel?

....

Q5   The extraction and processing of crude oil is a major industry.

a) Give one problem associated with burning crude oil fractions as fuels.

....

....

b) Name one product of the crude oil industry, other than a fuel.

....

Q6   An electric current is passed through acidified **water**, as shown in the diagram.

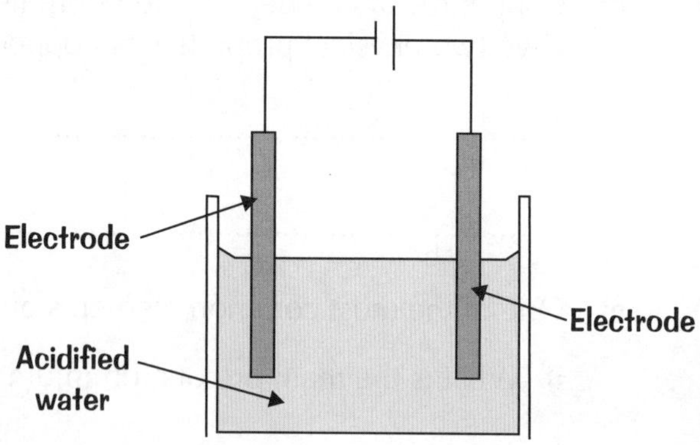

a) What is this process called?

....

b) i) Give the two products of this process.

1. ....

2. ....

ii) Give the chemical tests for these two products.

1. ....

2. ....

Mixed Questions — C1b Topics 3, 4 & 5

Q7   **Alkenes** are a type of hydrocarbon.

a)   The structural formula for ethene is shown in the box below.
Draw the structural formula for propene in the other box.

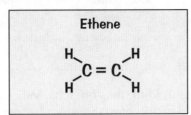

Ethene

Propene

b)   How do alkenes differ from alkanes?

....

Q8   Octane is broken down into hexane and ethene by heating it and passing it over a catalyst.

octane → hexane + ethene

a)   What is the process of splitting up long-chain hydrocarbons using heat called?

....

b)   **Decane** ($C_{10}H_{22}$) is cracked to produce **propene**.
Write a symbol equation to show this.

symbol equation: ....

Q9   Ethene molecules can join together in a **polymerisation** reaction.

a)   **Explain** the term '**polymerisation**'.

....

....

b)   Chloroethene molecules can also join together to form a polymer.
Name this polymer and **draw** a diagram of part of it below.

....

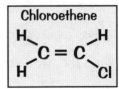

Chloroethene

c)   **Plastics** are polymers. Most plastics aren't biodegradable. Explain one problem this creates.

....

Mixed Questions — C1b Topics 3, 4 & 5

Q10 The diagram shows the **pH scale**.

1	2	3	4	5	6	7	8	9	10	11	12	13

↑ black coffee   ↑ milk of magnesia

a) The pH values of black coffee and milk of magnesia are marked on the diagram.

    i) Is black coffee neutral, acidic or alkaline? ....

    ii) Is milk of magnesia neutral, acidic or alkaline? ....

b) Indigestion is caused by the production of excess acid in the stomach. Milk of magnesia is used as an indigestion remedy. It contains a suspension of magnesium hydroxide, $Mg(OH)_2$. Explain how milk of magnesia can help with indigestion.

....

....

Q11 Some solid **magnesium oxide** was added to **hydrochloric acid** solution in a test tube. The incomplete word equation is shown below.

magnesium oxide + hydrochloric acid → .... + water

a) **i)** Fill in the name of the missing product in the space above.

    ii) What is this type of reaction known as?

....

b) When solid magnesium oxide was added to a substance **S**, magnesium sulfate and water were formed. Identify **S** by name or formula.

....

c) Circle the correct word in the sentence below.

Metal oxides and metal hydroxides are usually **acids / bases**.

Q12 Anass reacts **calcium carbonate** with hydrochloric acid.

a) Give the word equation for this reaction.

....

b) Describe how Anass could test for the gas produced in this reaction.

....

....

Changing Ideas About the Solar System

Q1 a) Tick the boxes to show whether the sentences are true or false.

True False

    i) Waves can be used to find out information about the Universe. ☐ ☐

    ii) We can observe stars and planets because they both give out visible light. ☐ ☐

    iii) Telescopes are our only method of observing visible light from the Universe. ☐ ☐

    iv) The invention of the telescope helped increase our knowledge of our Solar System. ☐ ☐

b) Write a correction for each false sentence.

....

....

....

Q2 Match up the descriptions with the correct method of observing the Universe. Each description might match more than one method.

Only really useful for mapping positions, e.g. of stars

Earth-based telescopes

Can be used to magnify images

Allow distant objects to be seen in more detail

Naked-eye observations

Observations can be made more difficult by light pollution and the Earth's atmosphere

Q3 Give **three advantages** of using **photography** to observe the Universe, compared with using telescopes or the naked eye.

    1. ....

    2. ....

    3. ....

Q4 Describe the main features of the **geocentric model** of the Solar System. Include a sketch of the model in your answer.

....

....

....

Changing Ideas About the Solar System

Q5 Our ideas about the structure of the Solar System have changed over time.

a) Complete the following sentences.

> **i)** The heliocentric model states that all the .... orbit
>
> the ....
>
> **ii)** The orbits in the heliocentric model are all perfect ....
>
> **iii)** In the heliocentric model the .... is at the centre of the Universe.

b) Give **one** difference between our current model of the Solar System and the heliocentric model.

....

....

c) Briefly describe how telescopes in general have helped change our ideas about the Solar System.

....

....

....

....

An egocentric model.

Q6 Galileo made some observations of Jupiter using a telescope that helped to provide evidence for the heliocentric model of the Solar System.

a) Briefly describe what Galileo saw when making his observations of Jupiter.

....

....

....

b) Explain how Galileo's observations helped provide evidence to disprove the geocentric model.

....

....

....

....

Waves — Basic Principles

Q1 Complete the sentence using the words given below. You will not have to use all the words.

matter   all   frequency   some   energy

.... waves transfer .... and information

without transferring ....

Q2 Here are **two ways** in which you can make waves on a **slinky** spring.

① ②

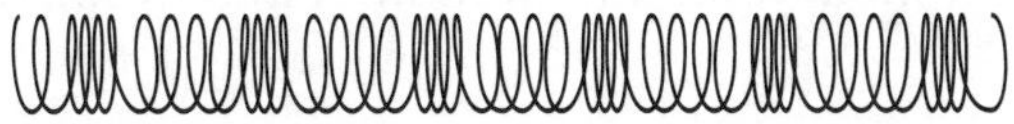

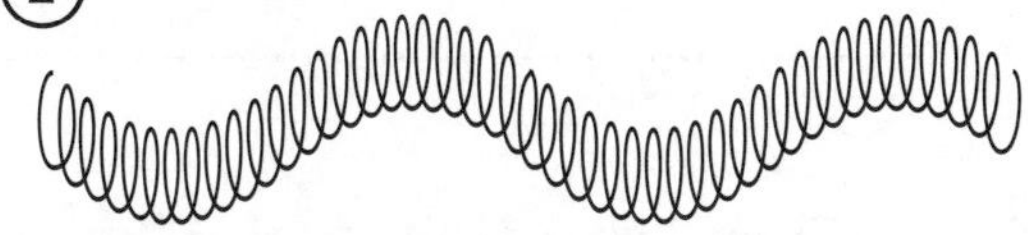

Which diagram shows a **transverse** wave, and which one shows a **longitudinal** wave?

Transverse: ....   Longitudinal: ....

Q3 Sort the waves below into two groups — **longitudinal** waves and **transverse** waves.

sunlight   'push-pull' wave on a slinky   S-waves   'shake' wave on a slinky

ultrasound   P-waves   electromagnetic (EM)   birdsong   drumbeat

Longitudinal: ....

....

Transverse: ....

....

Q4 Diagrams A, B and C represent **electromagnetic waves**.

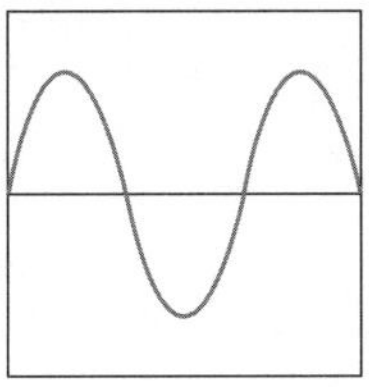

A 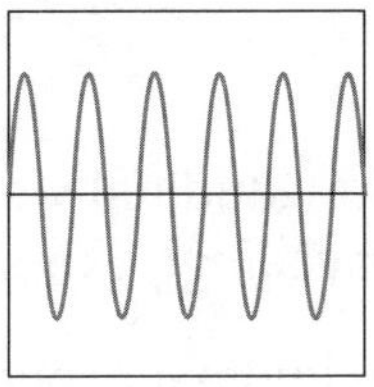   **B** 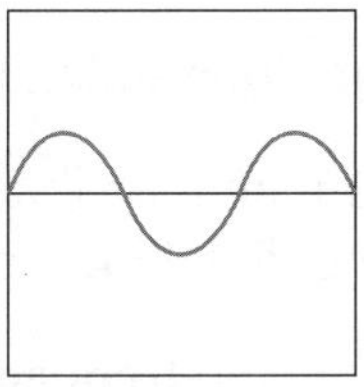   **C**

a) Which two diagrams show waves with the same **frequency**?   ...... and ......

b) Which two diagrams show waves with the same **amplitude**?   ...... and ......

c) Which two diagrams show waves with the same **wavelength**?   ...... and ......

Waves — Basic Principles

Q5 The crest of a wave travels 12 m in 5 seconds. Calculate the **speed** of the wave.

....

....

Q6 A ripple in a pond travels at **0.5 m/s**. It makes a duck bob up and down **twice every second**.

a) What is the **frequency** of the duck's bobbing? ....

b) When the duck is on the crest of a wave, **how far away** is the next crest?

Remember what's meant by a wavelength, then use $v = f \times \lambda$.

....

Q7 **Green light** travels at 3×10^8 m/s and has a wavelength of about 5×10^{-7} m.

Calculate the **frequency** of green light. Give the correct unit in your answer.

You'll have to use $v = f \times \lambda$.

....

....

Q8 The graph on the right is a representation of a **sound wave**.

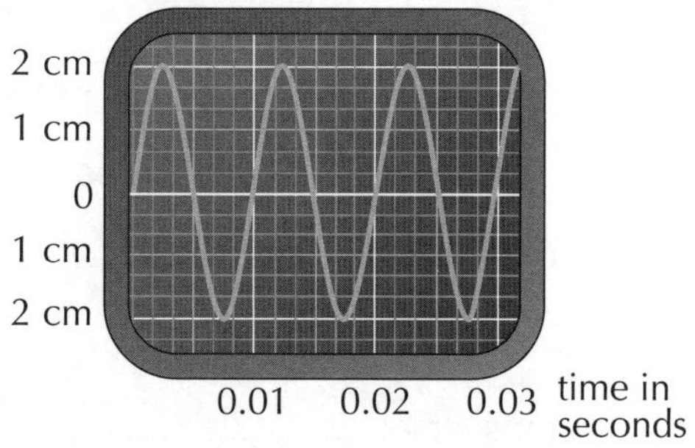

a) What is the **amplitude** of the wave shown by the graph?

....

2 cm
1 cm
0
1 cm
2 cm

0.01   0.02   0.03   time in seconds

b) How many **complete** vibrations are shown? ....

c) **How long** does it take to make each vibration? ....

Q9 Sound waves are **longitudinal** waves.

a) Which **direction** are the vibrations in a longitudinal wave, compared to the direction the wave is **travelling**? ....

b) What is meant by the **frequency** of a longitudinal / sound wave?

....

Top Tips: Woah, those last couple of pages were a bonanza of wave questions. As per usual, it's all really important stuff. Make sure you're happy with what is meant by the frequency, wavelength, amplitude and speed of a wave. And know how to rearrange and use the wave speed equations too.

Reflection and Refraction

Q1 Harriet spends at least an hour looking at herself in a **mirror** every day. The image she sees is formed from light reflected by the mirror.

a) What is meant by a "normal" when talking about reflection?

....

....

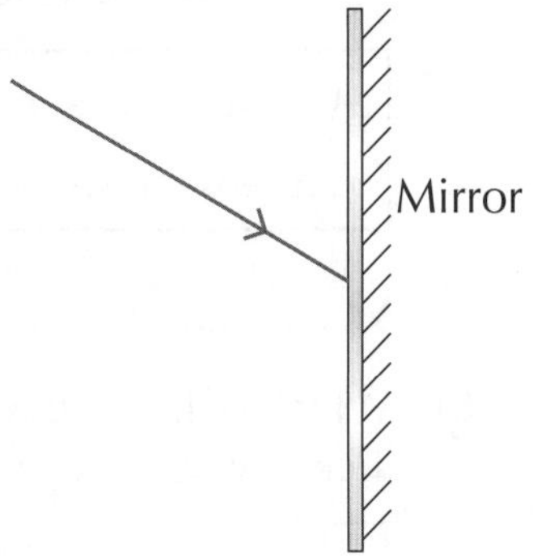

b) Complete the diagram to show an incident ray of light being reflected by the mirror. Label the **angle of incidence ,i**, the **normal**, and the **angle of reflection, r**.

Mirror

Q2 What causes **light** to be **refracted**? Tick the correct box.

☐ Refraction is caused by an image being formed at the boundary between two media.

☐ Refraction is caused by light being reflected off the boundary between two media.

☐ Refraction is caused by one medium being better able to absorb light than another.

☐ Refraction is caused by light changing speed as it enters another medium.

Q3 Jo is looking at a pebble lying on the bottom of a **pool**.

a) Does the bottom of the pool appear to be **nearer** to Jo or **further away** from her than it actually is?

....

b) Does light travel **faster** or **more slowly** in air than in water?

....

Q4 The diagram shows a light ray passing through **air** and through **glass**.

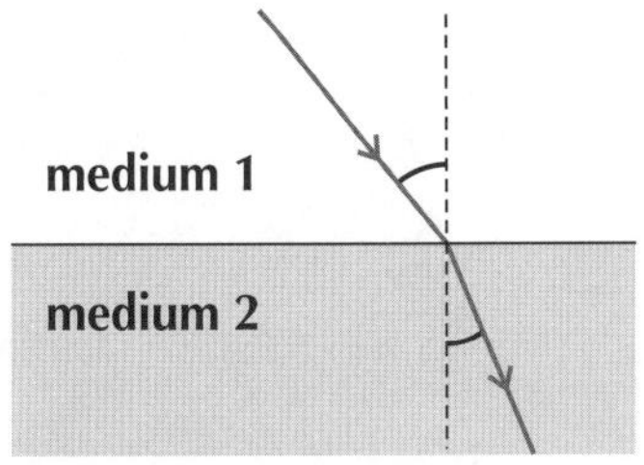

medium 1

medium 2

a) Fill in the gaps in this sentence to say which medium is **air** and which is **glass**.

Medium 1 in the diagram is .... and **medium 2** is ....

b) **Explain** your answer to part **a)**.

....

....

Lenses

Q1   Converging lenses are used to focus light.

a)   In the following sentences the words **parallel**, **converging**, **focal point** and **incident** have been replaced by the letters **W**, **X**, **Y**, **Z**. Write down which words are represented by **W**, **X**, **Y** and **Z**.

> *A(n)* **W** *ray passing through the centre of a* **X** *lens from any angle carries on in the same direction.*
> *A* **X** *lens causes all* **W** *rays* **Y** *to the axis to meet at the* **Z***.*

W .... X .... Y .... Z ....

b)   Which of the following incident rays do not have their direction changed by a lens?
Tick any boxes which apply.

☐ Any ray parallel to the axis   ☐ Any ray passing through the centre of the lens

☐ Any ray passing along the axis   ☐ Any ray passing through the focal point

Q2   Some of this diagram has been hidden. Draw in the rest of the diagram, showing the position of the **object** that produced the image you see.

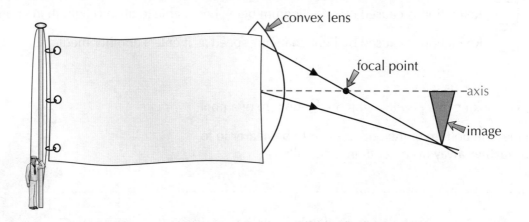

Q3   Briefly describe an **experiment** which could be used to work out the **focal length** of a lens. You may include a sketch in your answer.

....

....

....

Lenses

Q4 Gavin is carrying out an experiment to investigate the factors that affect the **magnification** of a converging lens. He wants to find out how an object's **distance from the lens** affects the image he sees.

a) Briefly describe how he could carry out this investigation. Your description should include all the equipment he should use.

....

....

....

....

....

....

The results from Gavin's experiment are shown in the table below, where F is the focal point of the lens.

Distance from lens to object	Distance from lens to image	Type of image	Size of image
Greater than 2F	Between 2F and F	Real, inverted	Smaller than object
Equal to 2F		Real, inverted	
Between 2F and F	Greater than 2F		
Less than F	Greater than 2F		Larger than object

b) Fill in the blanks in the table.

c) An object has a height of 1 cm. It stands on the axis of a converging lens, 5 cm away from it. The focal length of the lens (distance from the lens to the focal point) is 2.5 cm.

i) What size will the image be?

....

ii) Where will the image be formed, relative to the lens and the object?

....

Top Tips: In the exam, you might have to **describe** how to carry out a particular experiment. This means you'll have to list the **apparatus** needed and write a **detailed method** for the investigation. Make sure you list every little thing you might need — the examiners aren't mind readers. You might be expected to say what results you'd find too — but don't panic, it'll all be about stuff you've learnt. Yay.

Simple and Reflecting Telescopes

Q1 The following ray diagram shows light rays from an object in space entering a **simple telescope**.

a) Complete the diagram by labelling:
   i) where a **real image** will be formed,
   ii) the **eyepiece** lens.

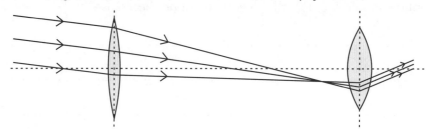

b) Explain how the eyepiece lens **magnifies** the image of a distant object produced by the objective lens.

....

....

....

Q2 Reflecting telescopes are made up of concave mirrors and a converging lens. The diagram below shows an example of a reflecting telescope.

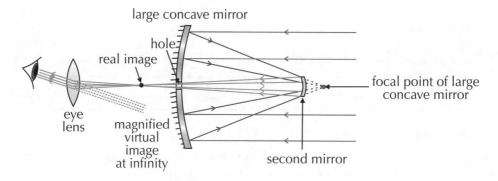

a) Explain what each of the following parts of the telescope are for:

   i) Large concave mirror: ....

   ....

   ii) Second smaller mirror: ....

   ....

b) Explain why there is a hole in the large concave mirror.

....

....

Electromagnetic Waves

Q1 Tick the boxes to show whether the following statements are **true** or false.

True   False

a) All EM waves are transverse waves. ☐ ☐

b) Radio waves have the shortest wavelength of all EM waves. ☐ ☐

c) All EM waves can travel through space. ☐ ☐

Q2 The table below shows the different possible wavelengths of EM radiation.

Complete the table to show the seven types of EM waves:

			VISIBLE LIGHT			
1m-10^4m	10^{-2}m (3 cm)	10^{-5}m (0.01 mm)	10^{-7}m	10^{-8}m	10^{-10}m	10^{-12}m

Q3 Red and violet are at opposite ends of the spectrum of **visible** light.
Describe two things they have in **common** and two ways in which they **differ**.

Similarities ....

....

Differences ....

....

Q4 Visible light waves with a wavelength of 10^{-7} m travel at 3×10^8 m/s in a vacuum.
Use this information to answer the questions below.

a) How fast would radio waves with a wavelength of 250 m travel through a vacuum?

....

b) Explain your answer to part **a)**.

....

....

Top Tips: Remember that you need to know the electromagnetic spectrum inside out — you might be asked to list the different types of EM radiation in order of wavelength or frequency. Don't forget that all the different radiations form a continuous spectrum — very high frequency radio waves aren't really very different from very low frequency microwaves.

Electromagnetic Waves

Q5   Circle the correct words to complete the following sentences.

While carrying out an experiment shining **sunlight/lasers** through a **lens/prism**,

Herschel discovered **ultraviolet/infrared** radiation. His experiment was designed to measure

the **temperature/wavelength** of the different colours of light. He noticed that his measurements

increased/decreased from violet to red. He took a measurement just beyond the red end of the

visible light spectrum and found that it was even **colder/hotter** than the red light.

Q6   Ritter discovered a type of invisible radiation using similar apparatus to that shown below.

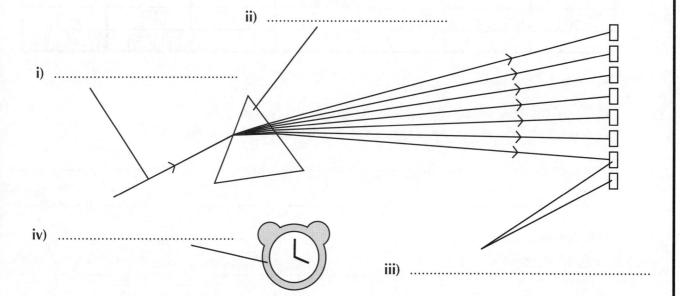

ii) ....

i) ....

iv) ....

iii) ....

a)   **Add labels** to complete the diagram above.

b)   Briefly **describe** an experiment to show evidence of this invisible radiation
      using the apparatus above. Explain what your results would show.

....

....

....

....

....

c)   What type of radiation did Ritter discover?

....

The Dangers of Electromagnetic Radiation

Q1 Here are four different types of **electromagnetic wave**:

visible light   microwaves   gamma rays   infrared

a) Which has the **lowest frequency**? ....

b) Which carries the **most energy**? ....

c) Which can cause damage by **ionisation**? ....

d) Which has the **highest frequency**? ....

Q2 Sunlight contains **ultraviolet radiation**.
Explain why excessive sunbathing can be **dangerous**.

....

....

....

Q3 EM waves with **higher frequencies** are generally more **damaging**.

a) Explain, in terms of frequency, why some **ultraviolet** radiation
can be almost as damaging as **X-rays**.

....

....

b) Give two effects that EM waves can have when they are **absorbed by living cells**.

1. ....

2. ....

Q4 Mobile phones use **microwaves**.

a) Why might people be worried that a lot of mobile phone use might be harmful?

....

....

b) Explain why it isn't safe to use infrared radiation for mobile phones.

....

....

Radio Waves and Microwaves

Q1 The house shown below receives **radio broadcasts** from a nearby transmitter, even though there is a mountain between the house and the transmitter.

radio transmitter

Use the words below to fill in the blanks in the passage.

ionosphere   direct current   short-wave   long-wave   alternating current   absorbs   reflects

The house can receive .... signals because they can bend

(diffract) around the mountain. It also receives .... signals

because they are reflected by the ....

Q2 Microwaves are used for **cooking** as well as for mobile phone **communications**.

Explain why your body does not get 'cooked' when you use a mobile phone.

....

....

....

Q3 Gabrielle in Britain and Carwyn in Canada are talking by mobile phone. The mobile phone signals are sent via a communications satellite.

Communications
Satellite

NOT TO SCALE

Carwyn's
phone

Gabrielle's
phone

Atlantic Ocean

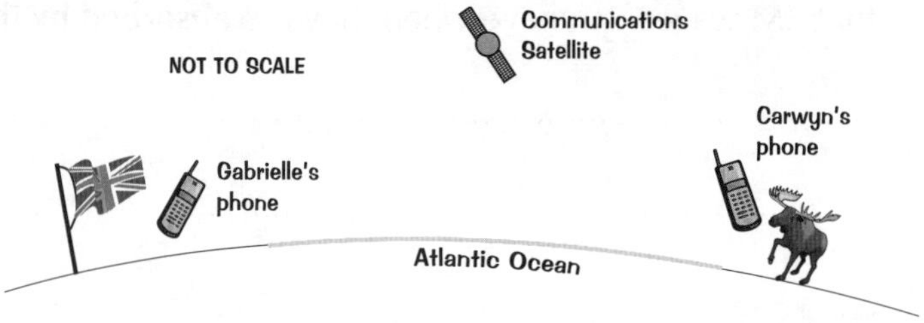

a) Suggest why the satellite needs to be high above the Earth.

....

....

b) Why are microwaves good to use for satellite communications?

....

c) Name another type of EM wave that can be used in satellite transmissions.

....

Infrared Radiation

Q1 Use the words in the box to **complete the paragraph** about **infrared** radiation.

| bright dark electrical heat hot night-vision |

Infrared is another name for .... radiation. People give out infrared because

they are .... The police use .... equipment to let them

see people in the .... The equipment changes infrared into an

.... signal which then appears as a .... spot on a screen.

Q2 Information can be transmitted quickly through **optical fibres**.

a) Tick the boxes to show whether these statements are **true** or **false**.

True False

i) Optical fibres carry electromagnetic radiation. ☐ ☐

ii) Optical fibres work because the EM wave is refracted along the fibre. ☐ ☐

b) Which of the following types of EM radiation is used in optical fibres?
Circle one answer.

Radio   Microwaves   Ultraviolet   Infrared

Q3 Infrared radiation has many uses.

a) Give two examples of appliances that use infrared radiation for each of the following purposes.

i) Cooking:

....

ii) Wireless communication between electrical devices:

....

....

....

b) Describe how infrared radiation is used in security systems.

....

....

Top Tips: The prefix 'infra' comes from Latin. It basically means 'below' — so infrared radiation is just radiation with a frequency below that of red light. The opposite of 'infra' is 'ultra', which means above or beyond — so ultraviolet radiation is just... You get the idea...

Visible Light, UV and X-rays

Q1   Eyes and cameras both use visible light in a similar way.

a) Briefly describe how we are able to see objects with our eyes.

....

....

....

b) Briefly describe how a camera forms and records an image.

....

....

Q2   **Ultraviolet radiation** is useful in detecting bank note forgeries.

a) What does a **fluorescent** material do when exposed to ultraviolet radiation?

....

....

b) Explain how banks can detect forgeries using **fluorescent ink** on their banknotes.

....

....

....

c) Explain why you might use fluorescent ink to mark your name on a valuable object, e.g. a laptop.

....

....

....

Q3   **Ultraviolet radiation** can also be used to make water safer.

Explain how this is done.

....

....

Visible Light, UV and X-rays

Q4 Explain why it is safe to use fluorescent lamps, even though harmful UV rays are produced inside them.

Q5 Choose from the words below to complete this passage.

| lead | plastic | bones | transmitted | soft tissue | aluminium | absorbed |

X-rays sent through a person's body can pass easily through .... but are .... more by .... Screens and shields made of .... are used to minimise unnecessary exposure to X-rays.

Q6 Indicate whether the following statements about X-rays are **true** or **false**.

True False

a) X-rays can be used to look inside objects. ☐ ☐
b) Medical X-ray photographs show "shadows of our bones". ☐ ☐
c) Flesh is more dense than bone so it lets X-rays through more easily. ☐ ☐

Q7 Describe two ways in which X-rays are used in airports.

1. ....
....
2. ....
....

Top Tips: Crikey, even more uses of electromagnetic radiation. The examiners are mad keen on you knowing all the different uses. So make sure you know all the examples on the last few pages. Some of them you might be really familiar with, but it's important to learn all the less famous ones too.

P1a Topic 2 — The Electromagnetic Spectrum

Gamma Rays and Ionising Radiation

Q1 Complete the following paragraphs on radiotherapy using the words provided.

ill	centre	normal	kill	cells	focused	cancer	dose	radiotherapy

High doses of gamma radiation will .... living .... Because of this, gamma radiation is used to treat .... Gamma rays are .... on the tumour using a wide beam. Damage to .... cells can make the patient feel very .... This damage is minimised by directing the radiation at the tumour and using the minimum .... possible.

Q2 Some rocks in the Earth's crust give out ionising radiation.

a) Circle the correct word below to show whether this statement is **true** or **false**.

Ionising radiation is emitted all the time from radioactive sources. **True / False**

b) Name **three** types of ionising radiation.

....

c) Explain what is meant by the term '**ionising radiation**'.

....

....

Q3 The diagram shows how radiation can be used to sterilise surgical instruments.

a) What kind of electromagnetic radiation is used?

....

radioactive source

thick lead

b) Similar machines can be used to treat fruit before it is exported from South America to Europe, to stop it going bad on the long journey. How does irradiating the fruit help?

....

The Solar System

Q1 Use the words in the box to **complete the paragraph**.

moons	Mercury	stars	Universe	Milky Way	Jupiter

The .... is made up of millions of galaxies. Our Solar System is in a galaxy

called the .... Each galaxy is made of billions of

.... Many planets have .... orbiting around them.

In our Solar System, the planets vary massively in size — .... is the smallest,

and .... is the biggest.

Q2 Even though the Earth's radius is a massive 6378 km, it's very small compared to the scale of the Universe.

a) Rearrange the following list of **astronomical things** into size order, starting with the smallest.

galaxy   moon   star   planet   Universe

.... ➡ .... ➡ .... ➡ .... ➡ ....

b) Fill in the table of **astronomical distances** with the **numbers 1-4**, to put them into the **correct order of size**. Make the smallest distance number 1 and the largest distance number 4.

	Distance between Earth and Sun
	Distance between stars
	Distance between galaxies
	Distance between Earth and Moon

Q3 Which one of the following statements is **not true**? Tick the appropriate box.

☐ The planets in our Solar System vary in size.

☐ The Sun is the largest object in our Solar System.

☐ The Universe doesn't contain all of the galaxies.

☐ Our galaxy is larger than our Solar System.

Top Tips: The examiners really want you to be able to compare the relative sizes of the Earth, the Moon, the planets, the Sun, galaxies and the Universe — and the distances between them too. So if that last sentence wasn't a big enough hint — learn all that stuff and you'll be raking in the marks.

Is Anybody Out There?

Q1 Robot landers are sent to Mars to carry out **experiments**.

a) Name one type of experiment that a lander might carry out.

....

b) Explain **what** the experiments you named in **a)** are looking for.

....

....

c) Give an **advantage** of remote sensing, compared to landing a robot on the surface of a planet.

....

....

Q2 The diagram shows a (made-up) **space probe** called **Erik** orbiting **Titan**, which is one of **Saturn's moons**.

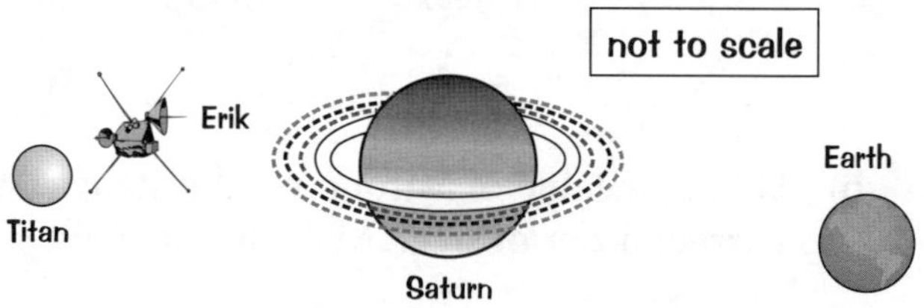

not to scale

Erik

Titan

Earth

Saturn

a) How would Erik **transmit data** back to Earth?

....

b) Give **one** example of the type of data the probe might collect about the moon.

....

Q3 a) What is the **aim** of the **SETI** project?

....

b) What **evidence** do scientists on the SETI project look for?

....

....

c) How can the **general public** help SETI with this?

....

Looking Into Space

Q1   The graph below shows the amount different
electromagnetic waves are absorbed by the atmosphere.

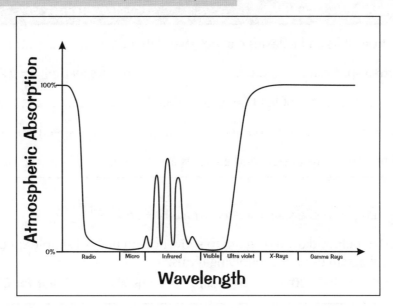

a)   Explain why X-ray telescopes are located in space.

....

....

....

b)   Give **one** example of something that has been discovered using
electromagnetic waves outside the visible spectrum.

....

Q2   Telescopes are improving all the time.

a)   How do we benefit from modern telescopes having improved magnification?

....

b)   Advances in telescopes and computers mean we are
now able to collect and analyse more data than ever before.
Explain the impact of this on our understanding of the Universe.

....

....

....

Space and Spectrometry

Q1 Use the words in the box to fill in the gaps in the passage below.

| elements | dark | slit | absorption | wavelengths |

Light from stars and galaxies can be passed though a .... in a spectrometer

to form a spectrum. .... lines in the spectrum are caused by certain

.... of light being absorbed by .... in the star's atmosphere.

Each element has its own particular .... spectrum, so spectrometers can be

used to find out what stars and galaxies are made of.

Q2 You can make a simple spectrometer from a box and a CD.

a) In the space below, draw a diagram to show how to make a simple spectrometer.
Label the diagram using the following terms:

CD   **light slit**   **eye slot**   **slot for CD**

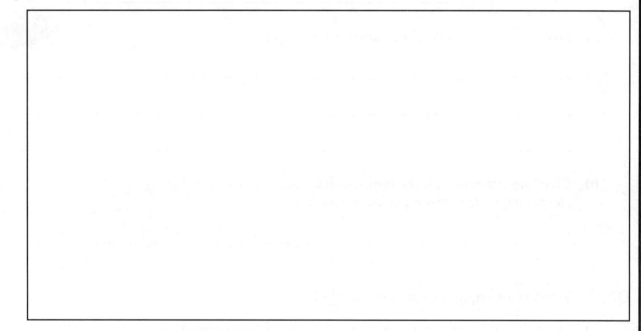

b) Explain why the spectrometer has to be used in a dark room.

....

c) An ordinary light bulb has a continuous spectrum because no frequencies of light are absorbed.
Circle the spectrum you would see through a spectrometer pointed at an ordinary light bulb.

The Life Cycle of Stars

Q1 A star in its **stable** phase **doesn't get bigger or smaller**, even though there are forces tending to make it expand and forces trying to make it contract.

a) What causes the outward pressure on the star?

....

b) What is the force pulling the star inwards? ....

c) Why doesn't the star expand or contract?

....

d) What is another name for a star in its stable phase? ....

Q2 Stars are formed from clouds of dust and gas called **nebulas**.

a) **Why** does the material come together?

....

b) Where does the **heat and light energy** emitted by a star come from?

....

Q3 Old stars eventually turn into **red giants**.

a) What causes a star to become a red giant? ....

....

b) Why is a red giant red? ....

....

Marilyn was nearing the end of her stable phase

Q4 Complete the passage below to describe what eventually happens to red giants.

A star with a similar mass to the Sun will eject gas and dust as a

...., leaving a dense core called a ....

A bigger star will explode as a ...., leaving a very dense core called

a .... The biggest stars will form a

.... instead.

Due to printing restrictions, red giants are currently unavailable.

The Origins of the Universe

Q1   **Complete this passage** using the words supplied below.

matter	energy	expand	explosion

Many scientists believe that the Universe started with all the ....

and .... in one small space.

There was a huge ...., and space and the material in it started

to ....

Q2   The '**Big Bang**' and '**Steady State**' theories are two theories of the origin of the Universe.

a) Briefly explain the idea behind the Steady State theory.

....

....

b) What does this theory suggest is happening as the Universe is expanding?

....

....

Q3   Francesca is standing by a busy street when an ambulance rushes past, sirens blaring.

a) As the ambulance moves away, how will the siren sound different to Francesca?
Underline the correct answer.

It will sound higher pitched   **It will sound lower pitched**

The higher the pitch, the higher the frequency.

b) Explain your answer to **a)** in terms of the change in frequency
and wavelength 'observed' by Francesca.

....

....

....

Q4   Which of the following statements is **not true**? Tick the appropriate box.

☐   Light from distant galaxies is at lower frequency than close ones.

☐   Galaxies further away from us have greater red-shifts than nearer ones.

☐   The light from distant galaxies has a lower wavelength than from those nearby.

The Origins of the Universe

Q5 Explain why the **red-shift** of galaxies provides evidence that the Universe is expanding.

....

....

....

Q6 The Big Bang theory and the Steady State theory are **two** models scientists use to explain the origin of the Universe.

a) What is cosmic microwave background (CMB) radiation?

....

....

b) Explain why the discovery of CMB radiation provided strong evidence for the Big Bang theory.

....

....

....

c) What other evidence is there to support the Big Bang theory? Explain your answer.

....

....

d) How does the Steady State theory explain the red-shift of galaxies?

....

....

e) Do **most** scientists currently accept the Big Bang theory or the Steady State theory as the model for the origin of the Universe? Explain your answer.

....

....

Top Tips: There are loads of different ways of asking about the origins of the Universe. But they all rely on you knowing the basic facts and different pieces of evidence. So know which bits of evidence explain the two big theories — the Big Bang theory and the Steady State theory.

Mixed Questions — P1a Topics 1, 2 & 3

Q1 The waves A, B and C represent **infrared**, **visible light** and **ultraviolet** radiation (not in that order).

Tick the box next to any of the following statements which are **true**.

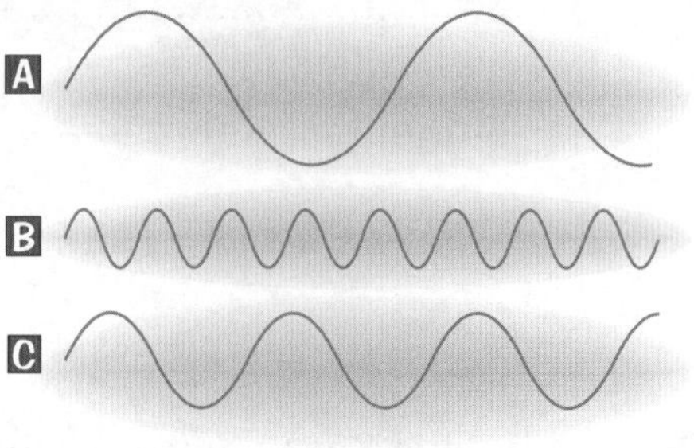

☐ B represents ultraviolet radiation.

☐ The infrared wave has the largest amplitude.

☐ C has the highest frequency.

☐ A has the shortest wavelength.

A

B

C

Q2 Infrared radiation is used by TV **remote controls**. Jake shows Peter that he can change the TV channel by pointing the remote control at a mirror on the opposite wall.

a) What property of EM rays has Jake demonstrated? Circle the correct answer.

reflection   refraction   diffraction

b) Draw a ray on the diagram below to show the path of the radiation emitted from the remote control to the TV.

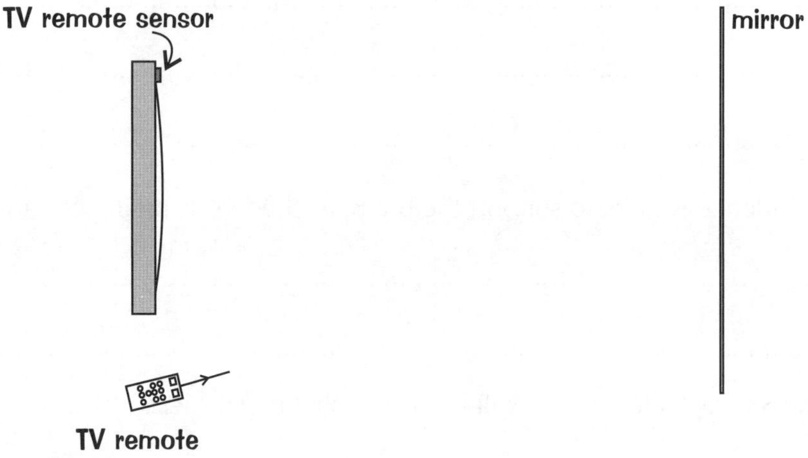

TV remote sensor

mirror

TV remote

Q3 A lander robot is sent to **look for signs of life** on Mars.

a) Describe one type of experiment that might be done by the lander.

....

b) The probe sends radio signals at a frequency of 95.6 MHz back to Earth. (Use $v = 3 \times 10^8$ m/s.)

Calculate the wavelength of the radio signals.

M stands for "Mega" and means "multiplied by 10^6".

....

....

Mixed Questions — P1a Topics 1, 2 & 3

Q4   The Sun consists mainly of **hydrogen**. It also contains **helium**.

a)   In a few million years time, the Sun will contain **more helium** and **less hydrogen** than it does now. Explain why.

....

....

b)   The Sun is currently in its 'stable period'. What determines how long a star's stable period lasts?

....

....

c)   Will the Sun ever become a **black hole**? Explain your answer.

....

....

Q5   EM radiation can be extremely **useful**.

a)   Using the boxes below, number the following types of EM radiation in order of **decreasing** frequency (1 = highest frequency). Write down one use for each type of radiation.

☐   Ultraviolet   ....

☐   X-rays   ....

☐   Infrared   ....

b)   SETI is an Earth-based project that searches for **narrow band radio waves** from space.

i) What does SETI stand for?

....

ii) Why are they only interested in narrow band waves rather than all radio waves?

....

....

c)   Explain how the **red-shift** of EM radiation produced by galaxies can be used to show that the Universe is expanding.

....

....

....

Mixed Questions — P1a Topics 1, 2 & 3

Q6 Radio Roary transmits **long-wave** signals with a wavelength of **1.5 km**.

a) Calculate the **frequency** of Radio Roary's transmission. (Use speed = 3×10^8 m/s.)

....

....

b) Mr Potts is on holiday in the Scottish Highlands. The cottage he's staying in has a TV and radio. Mr Potts loves 'The Archers' on Radio 4, but finds that he can only get long-wave radio reception. TV reception is also very poor, so he can't watch his favourite cookery and gardening shows.

Explain why Mr Potts gets **good** long-wave radio reception, but such **poor** short-wave radio and TV reception.

....

....

c) Mr Potts' holiday cottage has a microwave oven. The microwaves used in ovens are different from those used to carry mobile phone signals. Explain how they differ, and why different types are used.

....

....

Q7 Cancer is sometimes treated using **gamma rays**.

a) Describe how gamma rays are used to treat cancer.

....

....

b) Give **one** other use of gamma rays.

....

c) Exposure to gamma rays can also cause cancer.
Describe the link between the frequency of EM radiation and how dangerous it is.

....

....

d) Gamma rays are one type of ionising radiation.
Name **two** other types and explain what 'ionising' means.

....

....

Mixed Questions — P1a Topics 1, 2 & 3

Q8   Our ideas about the structure of the Universe have **changed** over time.

a)   Describe the **differences** between the geocentric model and the heliocentric model.

....

....

b)   Explain the role **Galileo** played in providing evidence for the heliocentric model.

....

....

....   *Galileo!*

....

c)   Briefly describe the ways in which **modern** telescopes have helped
us **improve** our understanding of the Universe.

....

....

....

....

Q9   Simple telescopes use **converging lenses**.

a)   Some of the light rays entering a converging lens in a telescope **refract**.
Explain what is meant by refraction.

....

....

b)   Describe how a **reflecting** telescope works. Include the following words in your answer:

large concave mirror   small concave mirror   focal point   hole   real image   eyepiece lens

....

....

....

....

P1b Topic 4 — Waves and the Earth

Ultrasound and Infrasound

Q1 Complete the following passage on foetal scanning using words from the list.

foetus	reflected	media	detected	echoes	body	image

Ultrasound waves can pass through most parts of the .... Whenever

an ultrasound wave reaches the boundary between two different ....,

some of the wave is .... back and can be ....   These

.... can be processed by a computer to give an .... of

the ....

Q2 Indicate whether the following statements are **true** or **false**.

Ultrasound waves have frequencies greater than 20 000 Hz.

X-rays are safe to use for foetal scanning.

Some animals use ultrasound frequencies to communicate with one another.

Bats use ultrasound to sense their way around an environment.

True False

☐ ☐

☐ ☐

☐ ☐

☐ ☐

Q3 Number the following sentences 1 to 4 to describe how submarines use sonar to detect things in the water around them.

	These ultrasound waves reflect off objects like other boats, the sea bed and marine animals.
	The reflected waves are detected as they arrive back at the submarine.
	The submarine emits waves of ultrasound.
	Computers on board time the delay between emitting waves and detecting their reflections. They then use this to calculate how far away objects are.

Q4 A boat is using **ultrasound** to scan the seabed. There is a **1 s** delay between the ultrasound being emitted and detected.

a) If the speed of sound in the water is **1500 m/s**, how far away is the seabed?

Use speed = distance ÷ time

....

....

b) If the boat passes over a **wreck**, what will happen to the time taken to receive the echo?

....

Ultrasound and Infrasound

Q5 Some animals use **infrasound** to communicate.

a) What is meant by infrasound?

....

b) Explain **why** some animals use infrasound to communicate.

....

....

....

c) Describe two other uses of infrasound:

1. ....

....

2. ....

....

Q6 Ultrasound waves are used in foetal scanning.
The speed of ultrasound in soft tissue in the body is 1540 m/s.

During one scan, it takes 0.000045 s for a wave to travel from the scanner to the baby's head and back again. Calculate the distance of the baby's head from the scanner.

....

....

Q7 A pulse of ultrasound is used to find the size of a large crack under the ground, through which water is flowing.

Convert everything to SI units first ($\mu s = 1 \times 10^{-6}$ s).

The two reflected pulses are detected 130 μs apart.
If the speed of sound in the crack is 1400 m/s, calculate the width of the crack.

....

....

....

Top Tips: Ah, a spot of maths to dust away the cobwebs. These pages should have given you lots of practice in working out the distance of something using ultrasound. Know what ultrasound and infrasound are — and their uses. Then you'll be set to pick up some juicy marks in the exam.

The Earth's Structure

Q1 The Earth's outer layer is made up of tectonic plates. Describe what causes tectonic plates to move.

Blame it on the boogie.

....

....

....

Q2 Scientists find it difficult to predict earthquakes.

a) What causes earthquakes?

....

....

b) Describe one method that scientists can use to try to predict earthquakes.

....

c) Describe the problems with the method in part **b)**.

....

....

Q3 Paula carries out the experiment below to show the unpredictability of earthquakes.

a) What will eventually happen to the brick as Paula slowly adds masses to the mass holder?

....

....

....

....

Elastic cord String Pulley

Brick

Sandpaper Bench Masses

b) Suggest what might happen if Paula repeated the experiment in exactly the same way. You should discuss how this is similar to a real earthquake in your answer.

....

....

....

Seismic Waves

Q1   **Draw lines** to match each of these words with the **correct definition**. One has been done for you.

seismic waves

seismograph

P-waves

S-waves

longitudinal seismic waves

shock waves from an earthquake

a device that records seismic waves

seismic waves that cannot travel through liquids

Q2 a)   Tick the boxes to show whether the sentences are true or false.

True   False

i) Seismic waves are caused by earthquakes and explosions.

ii) S-waves and P-waves can both travel through solids.

iii) All seismic waves are longitudinal waves.

iv) Seismic waves can be reflected but not refracted.

b)   Write out corrected versions of the **false** statements.

....

....

Q3   When there's an earthquake, **seismic waves** travel through the Earth.
S-waves and P-waves are two types of seismic wave.

a)   Why do both S and P waves **curve** as they travel through the Earth's mantle?

....

....

b)   Why do seismic waves abruptly change direction when they pass between the core and the mantle?

....

....

c)   Why are S-waves **not** detected at the Earth's surface immediately opposite the
site of the earthquake?

....

Top Tips: All the stuff on this page is fairly simple, but still really important. Make sure
you know what causes seismic waves. Learn about the two types of seismic waves too. Then reward
yourself with a pat on the head. Just the one though. We don't want you getting a big ego.

Seismic Waves

Q4 This **seismogram** shows the arrival of an **S-wave** and a **P-wave** after an earthquake.

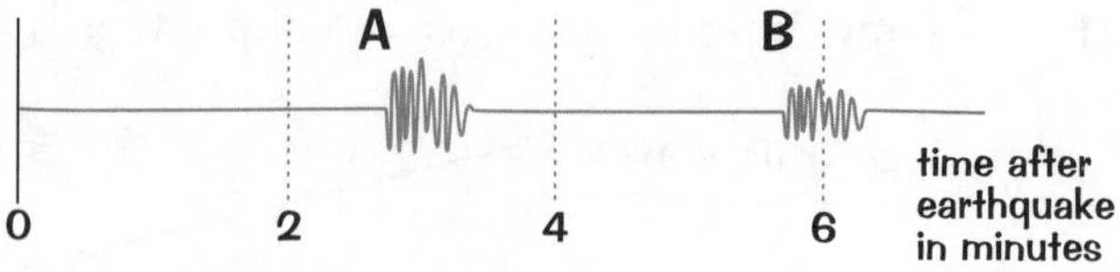

A   **B**

time after earthquake in minutes

0   2   4   6

a) Why do the two traces **not** arrive **together**?

....

b) Which trace shows the arrival of the P-wave — A or B? ....

c) The average speed of the P-waves is **12 000 m/s** through the mantle. Approximately how far was the seismometer from earthquake's epicentre?

wave speed = distance ÷ time

....

....

....

d) Describe two ways in which a seismogram recorded immediately opposite the site of the earthquake's epicentre would be **different** from the one shown above.

1. ....

2. ....

Q5 Seismograms can be used to work out the distance from a seismometer to an earthquake's epicentre.

a) Describe how three seismometers can be used to work out the exact location of an earthquake's epicentre. You should include a sketch in your answer.

....

....

....

b) Explain why at least three seismometers are needed to find the exact location of the earthquake's epicentre.

....

....

Electric Current and Power

Q1   Use the words below to fill in the gaps.

voltage   pressure   current   energy

> The rate of flow of charge around a circuit is called the ....
>
> .... is an electrical .... that pushes the current around
>
> the circuit. It gives a measure of the .... transferred.

Q2   Describe the **difference** between direct current (d.c.) and alternating current (a.c.).

....

....

Q3   The diagram shows three traces on the same **cathode ray oscilloscope** (CRO).
The settings are the **same** in each case.

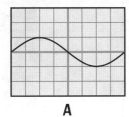   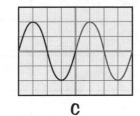   

A   B   C

Write down the **letter** of the trace that shows:

a) the highest peak voltage ....   **b)** direct current ....   **c)** the lowest a.c. voltage ....

Q4   **Fill in the gaps** using the **words below**. You might need to
use some of the words more than once, or not at all.

power   watts   current   what   how long   energy   voltage

Power is the .... transferred per second and is measured in ....

The total energy transferred by an appliance depends on .... it's used for and

its .... rating. The power of an appliance can be calculated using the formula:

power = ... × ....

Top Tips: Phew, lots of definitions on that page. To recap, know what current, voltage and power all are. Be able to explain the difference between direct and alternating current too. And don't go calling them d.c. current and a.c. current. Because that'd be direct current current etc. Chaos.

Electric Current and Power

Q5 Two filament lamps are plugged into a mains supply of **230 V**. **Lamp A** draws a current of **0.43 A** and **Lamp B** draws a current of **0.17 A**.

You'll need the equation which connects power, current and voltage for this question and the one below.

a) What is the power of:

i) Lamp A?

....

ii) Lamp B?

....

b) Which lamp is likely to be brighter? ....

Q6 The **current** an appliance draws depends on its **power** rating. Complete the table below, showing the power rating and current drawn by various appliances at mains voltage — **230 V**.

Appliance	Power (W)	Current (A)
Kettle	2600	
Radio	13	
Laptop computer		3.2
Lamp		0.17

CGP hide and seek tip #32

Q7 A simple experiment can be carried out to investigate the power consumption of a low-voltage **component** e.g. a lamp.

a) List all the equipment you would need.

....

....

b) Briefly describe how you would carry out the experiment, and how you would then use the data collected to calculate the power of the component.

....

....

....

....

....

Generating Electricity

Q1   Use the words in the box to **fill in the blanks** in these two paragraphs about generating electricity.

| moving | electromagnetic | magnet | coil | induction |
| alternating | voltage | reverses | magnetic | complete |

You can create a .... across an electrical conductor by .... a

magnet near the conductor. This is called ....

In generators, this is usually achieved by rotating a .... near a

.... of wire. The generator produces an .... current when it is

connected up to a .... circuit. The current alternates since the direction of the

.... field .... every time the magnet rotates by half a turn.

Q2   The diagram on the right shows the trace produced
when a **coil** is connected to a cathode ray oscilloscope
and a **magnet** is **rotated nearby**.

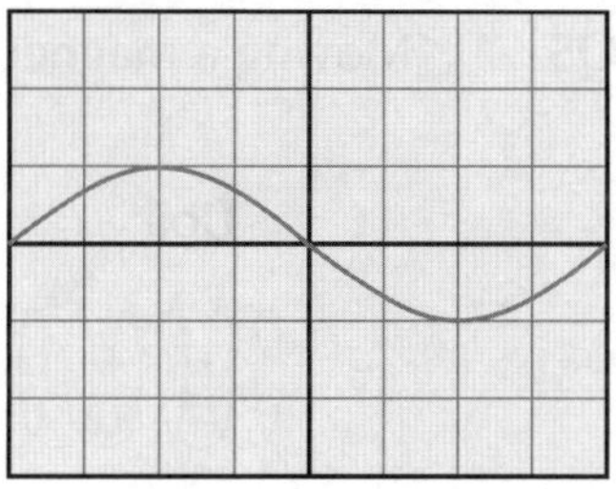

a)   On the diagram, draw what the trace would look like
if the magnet was rotated **faster**.

The amplitude and the frequency would change.

b)   Apart from rotating the magnet faster, what **three other things**
could you do to make the maximum current **larger**?

1. ....

2. ....

3. ....

Q3   The lights on Sebastian's bicycle are powered by a **dynamo**.
Explain why the bicycle lights dim as he slows down.

....

....

....

Top Tips: You can tell why people thought electricity was magic in the olden days — wave a
magnet near some wire and hey presto... you get some electricity. Make sure you know what to change
to make the voltage generated change and you'll generate lots of marks.

Generating Electricity

Q4   Decide whether the following a.c. generators would produce a **larger**, a **smaller** or **the same** current as the generator in the box. Circle the correct answer.

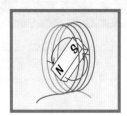

a)   larger / smaller / the same

b)   larger / smaller / the same

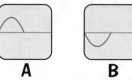

c)   larger / smaller / the same

Q5   Moving a **magnet** inside a **coil of wire** produces a trace on a cathode ray oscilloscope.

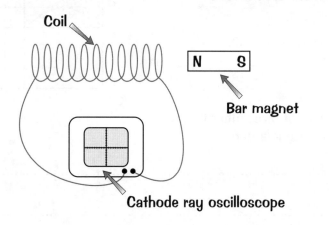

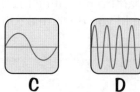

Traces on oscilloscope

A   B

C   D

When the magnet was pushed inside the coil, trace A was produced on the screen.

a)   Explain how trace B could be produced.

....

....

b)   Explain how trace C could be produced.

....

....

c)   Explain how trace D could be produced.

....

....

Non-Renewable Energy and Power Stations

Q1 The three fossil fuels, coal, oil and gas, are 'non-renewable' energy sources.

a) Explain what 'non-renewable' means, in terms of energy resources.

....

....

b) How do the start-up times for fossil fuel power stations compare with nuclear power station start-up times?

....

Q2 Nuclear power is another example of a non-renewable energy resource.

a) Give **one** advantage of nuclear power.

....

b) Why is nuclear power so expensive?

....

....

Q3 Match up each environmental problem below with something that causes it.

Acid rain

Climate change

Dangerous radioactive waste

Spoiling of natural landscapes

Releasing CO_2 by burning fossil fuels

Coal mining

Sulfur dioxide formed by burning oil and coal

Using nuclear power

Q4 Lisa says: "Using nuclear power to make electricity is too dangerous."
Ben says: "Using fossil fuels is even more dangerous in the long run."

Who do you think is right? Explain your answer.

....

....

....

Using Renewable Energy Resources (1)

Q1 Explain what 'renewable' means, in terms of energy resources.

....

....

Q2 Tick the boxes to show whether each statement applies to **hydroelectric** power or **tidal** power or **both**.

Hydro Tidal

a) Is usually used in estuaries. ☐ ☐

b) Is a reliable way to generate electricity. ☐ ☐

c) It can provide an immediate response to increased electricity demand. ☐ ☐

d) It is used to generate electricity by spinning a turbine. ☐ ☐

Q3 **Tidal barrages** can be used to generate electricity.

What happens to make turbines go round?

a) Explain how a tidal barrage works.

....

....

....

b) Give one reason why tidal barrages aren't used in very many places.

....

....

Q4 Describe two possible problems with using **wave power** to generate electricity.

1. ....

....

2. ....

....

Top Tips: The advantage of revision is that you've got a good excuse to eat lots of biscuits. The disadvantage is that you have to revise for an exam. Boo. Talking of advantages and disadvantages — learn all the ones for hydroelectricity, wave power and tidal barrages. It's bound to be on the exam.

Using Renewable Energy Resources (2)

Q1 People often object to wind turbines being put up near to where they live.

a) List two reasons why they might object.

1)..

2)..

b) List two arguments in favour of using wind turbines to generate electricity.

1)..

2)..

Q2 Explain the advantages and disadvantages of using **solar cells** to generate electricity.

....

....

....

Q3 Tick the correct boxes to show whether these statements apply to generating electricity from **geothermal** energy, **biomass** or **both**.

	Biomass	Geothermal
a) Set-up costs are high.	☐	☐
b) Does not release CO_2.	☐	☐
c) Possible in any country in the world.	☐	☐
d) Reduces the need for landfill sites.	☐	☐

Q4 Explain why burning biomass is almost '**carbon neutral**'.

....

....

....

....

Comparison of Energy Resources

Q1   The city of Fakeville decides to replace its old coal-fired power station.
They have to choose between using gas, nuclear, wind or biomass.

Give one **disadvantage** of each choice:

a)   **Gas** ....

....

....

b)   **Nuclear** ....

....

c)   **Biomass** ....

....

Q2   Read the statement below.

"Tidal power is a **plentiful** and **reliable** source of energy."

Do you agree with the statement?   Explain your answer.

I **agree** / **disagree** because ....

....

....

....

Q3   Give two possible arguments **in favour** of nuclear power.

1. ....

....

2. ....

....

Comparison of Energy Resources

Q4 At a public meeting, people are sharing their views about hydroelectric power.

We should use hydroelectric power more — it doesn't cause any pollution.

Brian

And it gives us loads of free energy.

Hillary

But it makes a terrible mess of the countryside.

Sue

At least it's reliable — it always gives us electricity when we need it.

Liz

Say whether you agree or disagree with each person's view, and explain your reasons.

a) I **agree** / **disagree** with Brian because ....

....

b) I **agree** / **disagree** with Hillary because ....

....

c) I **agree** / **disagree** with Sue because ....

....

d) I **agree** / **disagree** with Liz because ....

....

e) Outline two **advantages** of hydroelectric power which were not mentioned at the public meeting.

1)...

2)...

f) Outline two **disadvantages** of hydroelectric power not mentioned at the meeting.

1)...

2)...

Top Tips: These pages should have given you a nice summary of all the different advantages and disadvantages of large-scale electricity production. Remember, both non-renewable and renewable energy sources have their good bits and bad bits. Just make sure you know them. And job's a good 'un.

Electricity and the National Grid

Q1 Number these statements 1 to 5 to show the order of the steps that are needed to deliver energy to Mrs Miggins' house so that she can boil the kettle.

	An electrical current flows through power cables across the country.
	Mrs Miggins boils the kettle for tea.
	Electrical energy is generated in power stations.
	The voltage of the supply is raised.
	The voltage of the supply is reduced.

Q2 Using **high voltages** in power cables means you need some **expensive** equipment.

a) Explain why it is still **cheaper** to use **high voltages** for transmission.

....

....

b) What equipment is used to increase the voltage of the electricity for transmission?

....

c) What is used to reduce the voltage of the electricity before it arrives at the consumers homes? Explain why it is used.

....

....

Q3 Give two reasons why people might have concerns about living near power lines.

1. ....

....

2. ....

....

Q4 The **primary** coil of a transformer has **25** turns. The **secondary** coil has **50** turns. Calculate the primary voltage, if the secondary voltage is **30 V**.

Drum roll please for the turns ratio equation...

$$\frac{\text{primary voltage}}{\text{secondary voltage}} = \frac{\text{number of turns on primary}}{\text{number of turns on secondary}}$$

....

....

....

Electricity and the National Grid

Q5   Each of the following sentences is incorrect.
Write a correct version of each.

a)   The National Grid transmits energy at **high voltage**
and **high current**.

....

b)   A step-up transformer is used to **reduce the voltage** of the supply before electricity is transmitted.

....

....

c)   Using a **high current** makes sure there is not much energy **wasted**.

....

Q6   A transformer is used to **decrease** a voltage from 400 000 V to 240 V.

a)   What type of transformer is this? Explain your answer.

....

....

b)   If the primary coil has 20 000 turns, how many turns does the secondary coil have?

....

....

....

....

c)   The number of coils on the secondary coil is reduced to 10. If the primary voltage and
the number of primary coils both stay the same, calculate the new secondary voltage.

....

....

....

Top Tips: Ooh, that turns ratio equation is very versatile. You can rearrange it in lots of
different ways. Make sure you know how to use it to work out missing voltages and the missing number
of turns on a transformer, as well as where and why transformers are used. Maybe make a brew first...

Energy Efficiency & Cost-Efficiency

Q1   Match up the quantities used for calculating electricity costs with the correct units.

The **power** of an electrical appliance.

pence per kilowatt-hour

The **time** an appliance is used for.

kilowatt-hour (kWh)

The **price** of electrical energy.

hour (h)

The **electrical energy** used by an appliance.

kilowatt (kW)

Q2   All the units in the list below are units of **energy**, except for one.

kilowatt   kilowatt-hour   kWh   J

a)   Circle the 'odd one out'.

b)   What **is** this a unit of? ....

Q3   The amount of energy an appliance uses depends on its **power** and the **time** it's used for.

a)   Calculate how many **kilowatt-hours** of electrical energy a **2 kW** electric heater uses in 3 hours.

Energy used (kWh)   =   power (kW)   ×   time taken (hours)

=   .... ×   ....

=   .... kWh

b)   Boris gets his electricity supply from Ivasparkco. They charge 7 pence per kilowatt-hour.
Work out the cost of the energy calculated in part **a)**.

Cost of energy =   price of one kWh   ×   number of kWh

=   .... ×   ....

=   .... pence

Top Tips: Make sure you use the right formulas for energy and cost. Remember to use the correct units for the cost formula — it's worked out using kilowatts, hours and kilowatt-hours. Simples.

Energy Efficiency & Cost-Efficiency

Q4   Mr Tarantino wants to buy **double glazing** for his house, but the salesman tries to sell him insulated window shutters instead. He says they are cheaper and more **cost-efficient**.

	Double glazing	Insulated window shutters
Initial Cost	£3000	£1200
Annual Saving	£60	£20
Payback time	50 years	

a)   Calculate the **payback time** for insulated shutters and write it in the table.

b)   Is the salesman's advice correct? Give reasons for your answer.

....

....

Q5   Two **washing machines** are on sale with the following labels.

Techno   *A-rated*
Power: 2 kW
Average time of cycle: 30 mins
Price: £420

Sudso 2000   *Under £400*
Power: 2 kW
Average time of cycle: 45 mins
Price: £380

a)   i)   What is the energy consumption (in kWh) for each cycle for **Techno**?

....

     ii)   What is the energy consumption (in kWh) for each cycle for **Sudso**?

....

b)   The Adejonwo family does **four cycles** of washing each **week**.

     i)   How much **energy** would they save in **one year** by using Techno instead of Sudso? Give your answer in kilowatt-hours (kWh).

....

     ii)   1 kilowatt-hour costs 8p. How much **money** would the family save in one year by using the more expensive machine?

....

     iii) What is the **payback time** for buying the more expensive machine?

....

     iv) If the Adejonwo family's washing machine lasts 6 years, would it have been **cost-efficient** to buy the Techno? Explain your answer.

....

....

P1b Topic 6 — Energy and the Future

Energy Transfer

Q1 Use the words below to fill in the gaps.

converted   created   conservation

The Principle for the .... of Energy says:

Energy can never be .... or destroyed — it's only ever

.... from one form to another.

Q2 Complete the following **energy transfer diagrams** to show the **main** types of energy involved in:

a) a gas cooker, ... → ....heat energy........................

b) an electric buzzer, ...electrical energy.......... → ....

c) a television screen, ... → ....

d) a wind-up toy car, ... → ....kinetic energy........................

e) a nuclear reactor. ....nuclear energy.......... → ....

Q3 The diagram shows a **steam locomotive**.

a) What form(s) of energy are there in the:

i) coal? ....

ii) hot steam (which powers the engine)? ....

b) Describe two **energy transfers** which take place on the locomotive.

1..

2..

Q4 Bruce is practising weightlifting.

a) When Bruce holds the bar still above his head, what kind of energy does the weight have?

....

b) Bruce had porridge for breakfast. Describe how the chemical energy in his porridge is transferred to the gravitational potential energy of the lifted bar.

....

....

c) When Bruce lets go of the weight, what happens to its energy?

....

Energy Transformations

Q1 Tick the boxes to show whether these statements are **true** or **false**.

True False

a) **Efficiency** is the proportion of energy transferred to **useful** forms. ☐ ☐

b) The **wasted energy** from a device is the energy it delivers that's not useful. ☐ ☐

c) The more **efficient** a device is, the more energy it **wastes**. ☐ ☐

d) The **useful energy** transferred by a device is never more than the **total energy** ☐ ☐
supplied to it.

Q2 Here is an **energy flow diagram** for an electric lamp. Complete the sentences below.

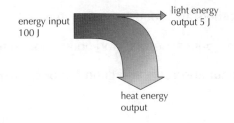

energy input
100 J

light energy
output 5 J

heat energy
output

a) The **total energy input** is .... J

b) The **useful energy output** is .... J

c) The amount of energy **wasted** is .... J

d) The **efficiency** of the bulb is .... %

$$\text{Efficiency} = \frac{\text{Useful Energy Output}}{\text{Total Energy Input}} \times 100$$

Q3 Use the **efficiency formula** to complete the table below.

Total Energy Input (J)	Useful Energy Output (J)	Efficiency (%)
2000	1500	
	2000	50
4000		25
600	200	

Q4 Tina was investigating a model **winch** — a machine that uses an electric motor to lift objects.

Tina calculated that, in theory, **10 J** of electrical energy would be needed
to lift a **boot** 50 cm off a table. She then tried lifting the boot with the
winch, and found that, actually, **20 J** of electrical energy was used.

Why did the winch use so much electrical energy in practice?
In your answer, include an explanation of what happened to the 'extra' 10 joules.

....

....

152

Heat Radiation

Q1   Tick the correct boxes below to show whether the sentences are true or false.   **True   False**

a)   The amount of heat radiation absorbed by a surface depends only on its colour.   ☐ ☐

b)   The hotter a surface is, the more heat it radiates.   ☐ ☐

c)   Good absorbers of heat are also good emitters of heat.   ☐ ☐

d)   Solar hot water panels use black pipes to reflect the heat.   ☐ ☐

e)   Silver survival blankets help the body to absorb heat.   ☐ ☐

Q2   Complete the following sentences by circling the correct words.

a)   Dark, matt surfaces are **good** / **poor** absorbers and **good** / **poor** emitters of heat radiation.

b)   The best surfaces for radiating heat are **good** / **poor** absorbers and **good** / **poor** emitters.

c)   The best materials for making survival blankets are **good** / **poor** absorbers and **good** / **poor** emitters.

d)   The best surfaces for solar hot water panels are **good** / **poor** absorbers and **good** / **poor** emitters.

Q3   Sue makes a cup of tea. At first, it is too hot to drink so she leaves it to cool.

a)   What can you say about the amount of heat **emitted** compared to the amount of heat **absorbed** by the tea, as it cools down?

   ....

   ....

b)   Sue forgets to drink the tea. The tea cools until it reaches room temperature. The temperature of the tea then stays **constant**. What can you say about the amount of heat **absorbed** and **emitted** by the tea now?

   ....

c)   Draw a line to match the beginning and end of each sentence below.

A system that's at a constant temperature...   ...radiates more power than it absorbs.

A system that's warming up...   ...radiates less power than it absorbs.

A system that's cooling down...   ...radiates the same average power that it absorbs.

Top Tips: Blimey, lots of definitions to learn. But it's really important you know them all. Now then, after all that I think we deserve a cup of tea. I'm parched, as my nana would say.

P1b Topic 6 — Energy and the Future

Heat Radiation

Q4 Tim did an experiment using a **Leslie's cube** to investigate the amount of heat different surfaces radiate.

Each surface on the cube had a different combination of **colour** and **texture**.

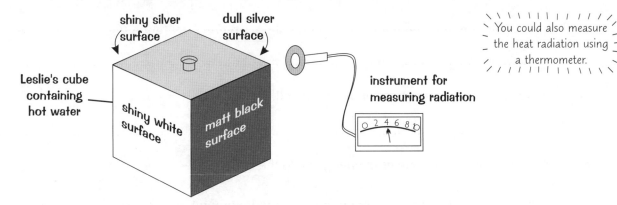

You could also measure the heat radiation using a thermometer.

Tim measured the heat radiation coming from each surface. His results are shown below.

Surface	Reading	Colour and Texture
A	10	
B	4	dull silver
C	4	
D	2	

a) Complete the table to show which was:

i) the **matt black** surface,

ii) the **shiny silver** surface,

iii) the **shiny white** surface.

b) Use Tim's results to write a conclusion for his experiment.

....

....

....

c) Which of the surfaces A to D would be best to use for the outside of a refrigerator? Explain your answer.

....

....

Mixed Questions — P1b Topics 4, 5 & 6

Q1   A group of farmers live on a remote island, growing potatoes and farming llamas. They decide to put **solar cells** on the roofs.

   a)   Suggest why the farmers have chosen to use solar power.

   ....

   ....

   b)   Describe the main energy transfer in a solar cell.

   ....

   c)   What other renewable sources of energy could the farmers use?

   ....

   ....

Q2   Dr Fergals has developed a new type of material, X, for **insulating** hot water tanks.

   a)   Dr Fergals tests the new material and compares it with fibreglass wool. Complete the table below.

Type of lagging	Saving per year (£)	Initial cost (£)	Payback time (years)
Fibreglass wool	14.56	60	
Material X	29.12	100	

   b)   Which material is the most cost-efficient? Explain your answer.

   ....

   ....

   c)   Make suggestions about the nature of the surface of the material X. Explain your answer.

   ....

   ....

Q3   Earthquakes cause **seismic waves** to travel through the Earth.

   a)   Say whether the following seismic waves are **transverse** or **longitudinal**:

   P-waves: ....

   S-waves: ....

   b)   Both types of wave curve as they travel through the Earth.

   Write down the name for this wave behaviour. ....

Mixed Questions — P1b Topics 4, 5 & 6

Q4 In one gas-fired power station, for every **1000 J** of energy input to the power station, 100 J is wasted in the **boiler**, 500 J is wasted in the **cooling water** and 50 J is wasted in the **generator**.

a) What **type** of energy is contained in the **gas**? ....

b) Calculate the **efficiency** of the power station.

....

....

c) Electricity generated in power stations reaches our homes by a network of power cables.

  i) Explain why these power cables are at very high voltages.

  ....

  ....

  ii) Explain why the very high voltages are not dangerous for people **using** the electricity.

  ....

  ....

Q5 There are some frequencies of sound that humans **can't** hear.

a) Write down the frequency range for each of the following types of sound waves.

  Ultrasound: ....

  Infrasound: ....

b) Ultrasound can be used to calculate distances.

  A pulse of ultrasound sent by a boat takes 3.2 seconds to travel from the boat to the sea bed and back again. If the speed of sound in sea water is 1520 m/s, how far away is the boat from the sea bed?

  ....

  ....

Use speed = distance / time

  ....

  ....

c) Give **one** other use of ultrasound.

  ....

Mixed Questions — P1b Topics 4, 5 & 6

Q6 A lamp is being tested in a circuit.

a) The voltage across the lamp is 6 V and the current is 0.5 A.
Calculate the power of the lamp.

....

b) Another lamp has a power of 40 W. Calculate how much it would cost to use this
lamp for 4 hours every day, for a week. The cost of electricity is 13p per kWh.

....

....

Q7 The diagram shows a **generator** that is turned by a wind turbine.

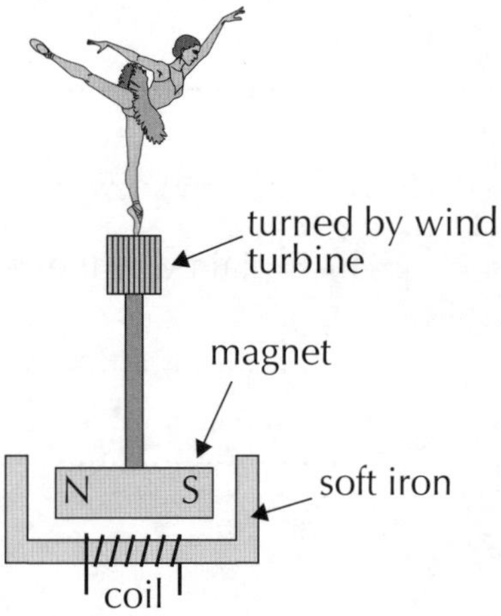

a) What happens in the coil of wire when the magnet is rotated
at a constant speed? Explain your answer.

....

....

turned by wind
turbine

magnet

soft iron

N   S

coil

b) The generator is attached to a cathode ray oscilloscope (CRO).

i) Circle the letter of the diagram that could show the output of the generator.

ii) Add labels to A and B to say which trace shows alternating current and which shows direct
current.

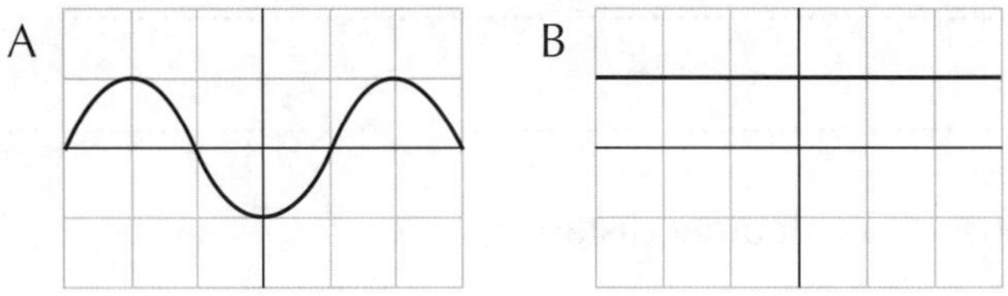

A   B

....

....

iii) Explain the difference between direct and alternating current.

....

....

c) Give one advantage and one disadvantage of using wind power to source all the UK's electricity.

....

....